Ken Cordier

GUARDIAN EAGLE
A Fighter Pilot's Tale

Colonel Ken Cordier USAF (Ret)

with Chris Snidow

GUARDIAN EAGLE

A Fighter Pilot's Tale

Colonel Ken Cordier USAF (Ret)

with Chris Snidow

Bible quotations come from the NIV translation, unless otherwise noted.

Colonel Ken Cordier USAF (Ret)
ken.cordier@sbcglobal.net
Tel: 214-942-3337

Book Cover painting by Cher Jiang
cher@chersfairyland.com
Tel: 417-388-1394

Chris Snidow
cowrind@sbcglobal.net
www.pilgrimwitnesses.com
Tel: 214-327-4579

Chris Snidow is the author of *The Witch That Wasn't-Joan of Arc and the God of the Bible* and *God is Working? A Whisper in the Storm.* Chris, and his wife Catherine, lead Joan of Arc Pilgrimages to France, and currently live in Dallas, Texas.

Table of Contents

Dedication

To God, the true 'Master of the Universe', for bringing me through an experience I could never have survived under my own strength and to the twenty-eight men who died in captivity in North Vietnam, having made the ultimate sacrifice while serving our great Nation.

Preface

It's not every day that you meet a real live 'Ken and Barbie' couple. My wife, Catherine, and I met Ken and Barbie Cordier in our Bible Study class several years ago. They both went out of their way to welcome us to the class. We noticed that they even looked a little like their famous namesakes. But that's where the comparisons with Mattel's famous dolls[1] stopped.

Barbie is a very warm person. She's bright, and obviously has exceptional 'social skills', but chooses to use them in a way to bring out others, as opposed to showcasing herself. Ken was the quieter of the two. He was simply but well dressed, low profile, listened to others, and seemed aware of things going on around him. There were no frills or attention-seeking behavior; just a quiet inner strength. At the time I first met him, I had no idea of his story.

Perhaps part of his laid-back nature goes back to his childhood church, the Church of the Brethren, a small American Protestant congregation. One of the hallmarks of this church is their emphasis on simplicity. In any case, it was only later that I learned about his amazing tale.

Ken's story is made up of intense suffering, courage, patriotism, triumph and a powerful God, always hovering protectively like an eagle above His beloved. I was surprised that Ken's story hadn't yet been put to paper. It's a story that needs to be told.

Ken has done the heavy lifting here, and for my part, I am happy that his story has finally found the light of day. May God be praised.

Chris Snidow
February, 2017

Prologue

"In a desert land He found him,
in a barren and howling waste.
He shielded him and cared for him;
He guarded him as the apple of His eye,
like an eagle that stirs up its nest
and hovers over its young,
that spreads its wings to catch them
and carries them aloft.'"
Deuteronomy 32:10-11

The eagle possesses great strength, fearless bravery, fierce independence and lifelong faithfulness. He is often used as a symbol of majestic beauty, and was adopted as the American national emblem in 1782. President Kennedy said, *"The founding fathers made an appropriate choice when they selected the bald eagle as the emblem of the nation. The fierce beauty and proud independence of this great bird aptly symbolizes the strength and freedom of America."*[1]

It is not surprising that the eagle frequently turns up in Scripture[2], sometimes as an analogy to one of God's good servants, but more often as an analogy to God Himself.[3] The above Deuteronomy passage is a good example of such a Guardian Eagle, and seems especially apt for Ken Cordier's story. In the war-plagued 'barren land' of Vietnam, Ken was miraculously shielded from death twice within one minute. Then once in prison, God cared for him. He never contracted a tropical disease, never lost his sanity, never gave up hope, never lost faith in God and Country, and eventually was lifted out of his life of suffering to one full of meaning, love and purpose.

The last four lines of these verses take on additional meaning when we take a look at the eagle's parent-child relationship. Unlike most animals, birds and many people, eagles are faithful to each other for the duration.[4] We see the value of faithfulness throughout Scripture. God is faithful.[5] He keeps His promises, and

11

we can count on Him (e.g. compare Gen. 12: 2-3 with the historical enemies of the Jews).

The parents build a safe and nurturing nest of thorns, twigs, soft grass and feathers to raise the eaglets. They know when it's time for their eaglets to get on their own, and they do what is necessary to bring it about. First, the mother eagle throws the eaglets out of the nest. Because they're scared, they jump back in. She takes off the soft layers of the nest, leaving the thorns bare, and throws them out again. When the scared eaglets jump back into the nest again, they are pricked by thorns. Screeching and bleeding now, they jump out on their own this time. Next, Mom chooses one of them for special attention. She pushes him off the cliff. Panic-stricken, you can hear him shrieking as he plummets to earth.

Meanwhile, Daddy has been keeping an eagle eye out (he can see another eagle soaring in the air up to 50 miles away!) on events below. He's ready for this moment, and uniquely equipped for it. He can dive at speeds up to 200mph—then pull up on a dime. Before the eaglet can crash to earth, Daddy dives down and catches him on his back, between his wings, and brings him back to the cliff nest. Then the process begins again.

Eventually the eaglet starts flapping his wings. Suddenly, he's flying! This 'sink or swim' approach (or rather 'fall or fly') is of course not really that at all. The father is constantly looking out for his child. The child is being prepared to face a dangerous world. Although he feels alone at times, in fact he never is. The analogies here are obvious, including these four: 1) our all-powerful Guardian Eagle loves us and is always looking out for us, even when we feel abandoned and alone. 2) we are being prepared for a dangerous world, and the one to come. 3) the Lord will help us to learn to fly. 4) trust in Him comes through practice and experience. Finally, Ken, as an eaglet in this analogy, has his whole life 'stirred up' and turned upside-down. He's rudely thrown out of his nest in despair and fear — falling, falling, then caught between the strong wings of his Guardian Eagle. He's taught to trust and fly, and eventually is carried aloft higher than ever before. This is his story.

Forward

VIETNAM – Setting the Record Straight

Who am I? Some say a hero but this is a very difficult mantle for me to assume. Although I made my way to the elite status of Air Force fighter pilot, checked out in the newest fighter in the USAF inventory (F-4C), and accumulated 175 combat missions, I was just one of thousands of pilots who flew combat in Vietnam [more than 8,000 US Airmen were killed] Although I flew some very challenging and harrowing missions, I was doing what I had trained for and found it very rewarding. In fact, I must say my months in combat were some of the most exciting, challenging and happiest times of my life.

Becoming a POW was no act of heroism either, and I certainly didn't volunteer for it! The POWs in N. Vietnam were a random sampling of all the pilots who carried the war to the North. If you put everyone's name on ping pong balls and shot them up like the lottery, a different mix would fall out, but the end result would be the same. This is because we all went through the same selection process and were trained to the same standard, so you could expect the same performance from another sample group.

Now, from the perspective of the passing of the years, I can see that the POWs, as a collective, have given the country a hero. Indeed, no argument that what we endured for our country was heroic. We were given a hero's welcome when Operation Homecoming brought us home to freedom in the spring of 1973. The whole country stayed up late to watch us step off the C-141s at Clark AB in the Philippines. Then we were feted with parades and local celebrations, culminating with the President's dinner at the White House. That was a wonderful time, filled with warm memories of the welcome of a grateful nation; something missed by the thousands of GIs who went to Vietnam and never came home, or when they did, were ignored, or worse.

Watergate soon eclipsed the Homecoming story, and we quietly assimilated into daily life and set about pursing our careers. I was asked occasionally to speak about my POW experiences, but usually only on the occasion of Memorial Day, Veteran's Day and POW/MIA Remembrance Day. Then, around the year 2000, I noticed a peculiar phenomenon: I was getting more and more requests to tell my story. I attribute this to the fact that the whole country has moved from the denial stage in dealing with our involvement in Vietnam to confronting our past by learning about what really happened.

The more I met with various groups, the more I realized that people not only knew very little about the events of the Vietnam War, but there were many misconceptions and false beliefs which have been perpetrated and reinforced by the mainstream media and Hollywood movie industry. This trend culminated in the 2004 presidential campaign when one of the candidates based his candidacy on his war record, most of which was largely embellished if not in part fabricated. The Swift Boat Vets took John Kerry to task through their ads depicting some of his more egregious claims, and in so doing changed the face of the political campaign. By way of a postscript, I was honored to play a part in their Number 2 ad.

The POWs were outraged by the conduct of Kerry when he returned to the states and was released from active duty. As you read on, you will appreciate why I and many of my fellow POWs could not stand by and watch a man who worked so ardently for our wartime enemy now become Commander-in-Chief of our armed forces. It's bad enough that he would become the United States Secretary of State. As I tell my story, you will understand why the POWs had such a visceral reaction, and why we endeavored to reveal the truth about Kerry's activities to the voting public through the documentary "Stolen Honor."

All this political activity was quite an epiphany for me, as my previous political involvement was limited to putting a yard sign out front of my home to support my candidate of choice. The real consequence of our involvement in the '04 campaign was the realization that there is a pervasive negative myth and lack of knowledge about the Vietnam War. This led to a decision to form the VVLF—Vietnam Veterans Legacy Foundation—with the broad goal to "set the record straight" about the war in Vietnam and the reputation of Vietnam Veterans. It also gave me an answer to a question which had haunted me ever since December 2, 1966 when I was shot out of the skies over North Vietnam: Why did I miraculously escape a close encounter with the grim reaper twice in less than a minute? I think I now have the answer: "for just such a time as this....."

"For Such a Time as This"

Chapter 1

"And who knows whether you have not come to the kingdom for just such a time as this." (ESV) Esther 4:14

It was just a little thump. Sort of a soft, dull thud. To the uninitiated, it could easily have been written off as 'accidental contact'. Coming from the adjacent room, it sounded kind of muffled; not very loud at all. But it didn't need to be. For me, the message was loud and clear.

I got up slowly, and silently took a couple of steps to the opposite side of my tiny 7' X 9' 'cell'. There, in my turn, I delivered a measured elbow bump to the wall. Just a little bump. I recognized and passed it on to the next cell. So it went, until all the prisoners in the building had gotten the signal. It was Sunday, and the thump signaled it was time for church. Who could have imagined that the service-announcing church bells of my youth would now be replaced with these little elbow wall-thumps?

By necessity, surreptitious ways of communication had been developed to a fine art here at Nga Tu So (or Ngax Tuw Sowr). Of course, the American prisoners didn't call it that. It was simply known as 'the Zoo'. Why the Zoo? Simply put, because we were kept in cages like animals. The guards would sneak around the camp and suddenly open the inspection hatch, trying to catch prisoners in unauthorized activities, which was anything but sitting quietly and 'thinking about our war crimes.'

The guards may have peeked in, but the prisoners also peeked out. There was a convenient crack under the door, and the ever-vigilant POWs tried to keep a close eye out for approaching guards.

All clear?

There were thirteen Vietnamese prisons used during the American involvement of the war (1961-1975), but the Zoo, along with the infamous 'Hanoi Hilton', quickly gained a reputation as one of the worst, due to the horrendous treatment of its inmates. men never gave up on God. And Sunday was still the day of the Lord.

As it was their day off, many of the guards were usually not around on Sundays. And this Sunday was no exception. After the SRO (Senior Ranking Officer) began the 'elbow-bells' process, and word was spread throughout the building, we'd all stand up and face East, which was the general direction of America. We'd whisper the Pledge of Allegiance followed by the Lord's Prayer. Then for approximately 10 minutes we could meditate, or discuss various aspects of our religion with our cellmate, if we had one. Of course, there was no preacher, no choir, no singing allowed. At the end of the simple service, the SRO would thump the wall again. It would go around the building, and then we'd all stand up once more and recite the 23rd Psalm. And that was the end of church for that week.

It was forbidden to speak in audible tones. We could only whisper to our cellmate. If the guards ever heard your voice outside the cell, they'd accuse you of communicating and come in and beat you up or worse.

After church, things reverted back to their daily routine, which most people can't even imagine. To get a glimpse of this daily life, we have to start with the environment itself

.

Located in the southwestern suburbs of Hanoi, the Zoo opened its' doors in September 1965, more than a year before Capt. Cordier's arrival. Coincidentally, beginning in late 1965 the application of severe torture against U.S. prisoners became commonplace. Unfortunately for Ken and his comrades, the conditions of captivity and treatment we'd receive for the next several years, would prove to be among the worst of the entire Vietnam War, and that's saying something.

As the camp authorities gained experience in dealing with the Americans, they bricked up all the windows in an attempt to prevent communication. Three things immediately resulted. First of all, the inmate's observable world was reduced to this claustrophobic 7'X 9'area. They didn't want us to see each other and communicate. In fact, it was forbidden to see other POWs. We were to be kept completely isolated.

"Secondly, it made the cells very hot. There was no ventilation. It was like an oven in those cells during summer with clay tile roofs. Guys like me like me with light skin would get heat rash. I learned why they called it 'prickly heat'. Those little red spots felt like pin pricks and it would get worse and worse. One day I tapped on the wall to the guy next door and asked, 'When does this stop?' He tapped back, 'When it covers you from head to toe.' The trouble was, these red spots would turn into pustules which would break and get infected and turn into boils.[1] One summer I had 47 boils, and of course we never had any medical attention. They didn't care. We were there to be punished. They weren't worried about our creature comforts.

"Thirdly, natural light would never penetrate these dank cells; no day light, no sunlight; no moon light, no starlight. Now, when we think of all the torture, starvation, cruelty and overriding fear applied here, this was quite likely the least of our day-to-day concerns. But light deprivation is no small thing.[2]

"When describing our cells, I use the "Five Bs". We just mentioned the first 'B', i.e. the bricks. The four others are: the boards, the bulb, the box, and the bucket.

"The boards were actually our bed. It was like a crude door on saw horses, just planks nailed together with no mat or mattress. Hanging over our bed was the third 'B', a bare lightbulb, which was on 24/7. You might think they would turn out the lights during the day, but the cells were dark and they wanted to peek in and see if we were doing something unauthorized.

"The fourth 'B' was 'the box'. There was a small speaker box on the ceiling in every cell. That was for our 're-education'. We had the Voice of Vietnam (a North Vietnamese radio propaganda broadcast)[4] in the morning and evening, and locally produced propaganda from the interrogators. Unlike Korea, where they had re-education classes, here they just piped the propaganda into the rooms, and the whole camp became a class room.

"The last 'B' was the bucket. The rusty bucket in the corner was our toilet, and they let us out once a day to empty it.

A typical Zoo cell (prisoner unknown)

"So much for home sweet home. I was to be in that camp for three years and eight months and never go more than 100 yards in any direction. Still, we never gave up hope, and we never lost our faith in God and Country."

Of course each camp, and each building in that camp, was different. But this was the reality of the Zoo in late 1966. As such, these men would find themselves in the middle of one of man's most-repeated themes: man's inhumanity to man.

There's something wrong with us. History, Scripture and the newspapers are full of countless examples of this age old curse. As we go through Ken's story, one can't help but wonder sometimes why the good Lord allows such atrocities to take place in the first place?

Many have attempted to answer this question, but the only answer that can satisfy comes from the Bible. Yes, there's something terribly wrong with us. It's a soul-sickness that the Bible identifies succinctly as sin.[5] Although the end of sin and death is coming one day[6], until then we remain in this netherworld between Heaven and Hell. The Zoo is decidedly closer to Hell. As we'll see, the Lord watches over His own. This will include Ken, languishing in various North Vietnamese prisons for years. God did not forget him. In His good time, He lifted him up and restored him much as He did with Job of the Bible.

We see evidence of the Lord providentially watching over His own in several places in the Bible. A good example is found in the book of Esther. Esther is an unusual Biblical book; one where God is never even mentioned outright.

Nonetheless, Esther's story[7] shows us how God's plans are often long range; sometimes spanning generations. Perhaps you can see some of His plans for you as you look back over your own life and family history? At one point Esther is told, "And who knows, whether thou has not come to the Kingdom for such a time as this." Esther 4:14 (ESV)

For such a time as this? Esther's whole life was leading up to a specific time, place and set of circumstances; a time pregnant with meaning. Surely many apparently insignificant things from her past contributed. The same must also be true for us, although no doubt applied differently in each case. Our suffering does have meaning and purpose[8], although often obscured from us at the time. Indeed, maybe we won't see, much less understand, much of it this side of Heaven.

Sometimes we do see the puzzle pieces being put together in our own lifetime. Capt. Cordier was a North Vietnamese POW for more than 6 years. When he was finally released and returned home, he'd find that his marriage was unable to survive such a long and traumatic separation. However, as we'll see, the Lord was not finished with him.

The incredible suffering of the Vietnam War, like all wars, didn't discriminate or take sides. There was enough to go around for everybody. But for just such a time as this, we'll take a look at what our brave American POWs had to endure, focusing on one particular airman: Capt. Ken Cordier, Fighter Pilot, USAF.

A Fun but Not So Easy Job

Chapter 2

"The ordinary air fighter is an extraordinary man and the extraordinary air fighter stands as one in a million among his fellows."[1] Theodore Roosevelt

"When I grow up I want to be a pilot because it's a fun job and easy to do. That's why there are so many pilots flying around these days. Pilots don't need much school. They just have to learn to read numbers so they can read their instruments. I guess they should be able to read a road map, too...The salary pilots make is another thing I like. They make more money than they know what to do with. This is because most people think that flying a plane is dangerous, except pilots don't because they know how easy it is. I hope I don't get airsick because I get carsick and if I get airsick, I couldn't be a pilot and then I would have to go to work."
From a fifth grade student at Jefferson School, Beaufort, SC. [2]

So, you saw *Top Gun*, and now you want to be a fighter pilot? O.K., no problem. Here are the 4 easy steps that Ken took. Just follow these, and maybe you, too, can become a fighter pilot:

Step 1- As a youngster, look at planes in the sky, and dream about flying them.

A 'coincidental' change by Ken's family would have long range impact on him. They moved to Akron, Ohio when he was 5 years old. They were there during WWII, when a division of Goodyear licensed and built the F-4U Corsair, i.e. F-4G. When one came off the production line, a navy pilot would crank it up, take off, and fly around the traffic pattern and land it. If they didn't have any problems with it, they'd turn it over to the Navy and deliver it. The traffic pattern passed over the Cordier house, so every day he'd see Corsairs flying over, dreaming of the day when he would be able to fly one himself.

A F-4U Corsair

Step 2- At a very young age, start making model airplanes and decide to become a fighter pilot:

A typical 5-6 year old boy,
making model airplanes.

As a young lad, Ken built many models of the Corsair and other airplanes of the day. Before plastic models, his models were painstakingly glued together using balsa sticks and tissue paper.

Step 3- Get rides in a real airplane.

A Piper Cub

Ken's first ride in an airplane was when he was around 5 years old. His uncle took him up in a Piper Cub, much to the dismay of his mother, who pitched a fit when she found out after they had landed.

Step 4- Become a fighter pilot in the USAF or the Navy.

Here's the real deal:
Now Colonel Ken Cordier, Fighter Pilot, USAF

See how easy it is? Ken followed these tried and true steps, and realized his dream. However, you may have noticed that the "4 Easy Steps" are not very detailed. And the devil is in the details. Let's take a closer look.

~~~~~~~~~~~~~~

The Six Million Dollar Man

"Steve Austin, astronaut. A man barely alive. We can rebuild him. We have the technology. We can make him better than he was. Better...stronger...faster." [3]

"The bulk of mankind is as well equipped for flying as thinking."
Jonathon Swift

Although many of us might get through the first three steps, Step 4 would prove to be our undoing, at least for most of us.

So how does one become a fighter pilot? Very few can make the grade. It is a specialty among specialists. Look at it this way: in the United States only one out of approximately every 22,400 actually end up becoming a USAF fighter pilot.[4]

Still interested? Here are some things to take into consideration. First of all, you must obtain a Bachelor's Degree, and then become an officer. Then you need to be selected into one of the following three officer commissioning programs: Reserve Officers' Training Corps (ROTC), the Air Force Academy (USAFA) or the Naval Academy (USNA).

How do they select candidates for the few places available? Here are some of the things they look for: physical fitness, an exceptional academic record, healthy well-being, strong character, mental drive, a strong heart, 20/20 eyesight, good sense of direction, strong leadership and teamwork abilities, and nerves of steel. So far, so good?

You would also need a healthy dose of the 'right stuff.' The Air Force has traditionally been fairly closed-mouth about what exactly the "right stuff" consists of. However, you must excel in absolutely everything you do from day one. You work to graduate at the top of your training class so that you have first choice of assignments. You also need instructors that like you enough to recommend you to fly a fighter. Finally you need good timing, so that the Air Force is actually looking for fighter pilots at the time of your graduation.[5]

Ultimately, you've got to be more than just determined and qualified. You must be open to change and adaptation. The world of aerial warfare is continually evolving. Today's fighter pilots are expected to be able to execute extremely complicated aerial maneuvers while dealing with g-forces (i.e. the amount of gravity forces they're physically feeling) that drain the brain of precious blood and could cause them to black out.[6]

Remember, as you fly around in this 20,000-lb. hunk of metal and jet fuel, the fighter pilot, at the touch of a button, has the ability to operate machinery that costs tens of millions of dollars, travels at supersonic speeds, and fires some of the most sophisticated weaponry ever created.

Of course, all of this specialized selection and training is very expensive. It costs the taxpayer about $6 million a year or more to train one fighter pilot in the Air Force today.[7] Fighter pilots are the real $6 million men of today. So, as you might imagine, the Air Force is rather particular about who they let play with their toys.

If you realize your goal and become a fighter pilot, you might expect that you would then make a lot of money. You'd be wrong. If qualified and selected, your starting flight pay would be around $150 a month on top of your regular salary.[8] This is not something you do for the money.

~~~~~~~~~~~~~~

Following Ken's 4 Easy Steps

"The air up there in the clouds is very pure and fine, bracing and delicious. And why shouldn't it be? —it is the same the angels breathe." Mark Twain[9]

As a boy, I dreamed of becoming a fighter pilot. I was building model airplanes by the time I was five or six years old, and played with a cardboard mockup of an aircraft instrument panel, which included a basic manual "How to Fly".

Unfortunately, I was a sickly child. Every year for 2-3 years I had a bad strep throat, and it infected my tonsils and my teeth. By the 3rd go around, when I was 10, I got rheumatic fever. That put me on bed rest for 3 months, and it really changed my life.

My mother was a very strong willed person. Fortunately for me, she enforced the doctor's instructions, and didn't allow me to be active. At this time, 1947, penicillin was just appearing in the civilian community, and I got weekly penicillin injections. What would now be a very low dose was a massive shot in my butt, and I remember it raised a bump that to me seemed the size of a walnut. That and the bedrest kept me from developing complications, so I didn't develop a heart murmur. However, that really affected my psyche, and how I thought. I had a lot of resentment and anger with a situation I couldn't control. I wasn't able to develop like other kids physically, since I was limited with regard to physical activities. By the time I was over this, I was a couple of years behind my peers, and physically never did catch up. For that reason I never developed much interest in sports, and to this day I'm sports apathetic. It was a major event in my life that affected me for the rest of my life. So that was a transition.

By the time I began my junior year high school, I had developed an interest in music and took trumpet lessons. In high school I participated in both band and orchestra, and did very well.

My grades were also good, but I never really applied myself. A kid from Latvia was very bright, and always made straight A's. We all knew that he'd be valedictorian, and I always assumed I'd be number 2, but I ended up number 3 in my class. What a surprise that was, and it taught me a lesson: pay more attention to things. That was kind of a reality check because I had assumed too much. There was a girl in my class who became number 2. She took a secretarial course, not any math or science, none of the hard courses, but she did what she did, and excelled. I wouldn't call that a life event, but it was a lesson along the way.

Then I went to college. Due to the influence of my father, I elected to major in engineering. That put me on a trajectory that led nowhere. I wasn't a good student in college. I ended up number 18 out of 54 in my class. So I was a B+ student at best. I just didn't do well in the engineering courses. I got all A's in the easy stuff like history and liberal arts courses. But I stuck with it. I was determined to get my engineering degree, and I did.

Along the way I took two years of ROTC. I had to choose a service, so I chose the Air Force, because I always wanted to be a pilot. In 1957, with the draft looming over my head, I decided to go into Advanced AFROTC. I knew that otherwise, as soon as I graduated from college, I'd be drafted. I couldn't see myself being a foot soldier toting a gun after beating my brains out for 5 years in engineering school.

In Advanced ROTC, I found out that I had a less than perfect depth perception, so I couldn't go to pilot training. However, I'd already signed up, so I thought I'd do my minimum service and get out. That was my plan when I graduated from college. Then I was assigned to the Intercontinental Ballistic Missile (ICBM) Minuteman training squadron, and spent a year there learning the Minuteman[10] weapon system. After a year of preparation I taught my first course, but in the meantime, I had my first annual physical, and made an offhand comment to the doctor: 'The only thing that kept me out of pilot training was my depth perception,'

He said, 'Oh, a lot of people have a problem with that test. I've got another test here.' I passed it 100%, so he said, 'There's nothing wrong with your depth perception.'

I applied for pilot training and after a lot of red tape, eventually got accepted. I reported to Laughlin Air Force Base in Del Rio, Texas in January 1963. I entered pilot training and soloed in a T-37. After completing the Primary Phase, I transitioned to the T-33, and in December of 1963, I graduated and got my wings. Once again, I was 3rd in my class, but I did get my choice of assignments.

I could have either gone to F-100s with training at Nellis AFB, or I could have gone to F-4Cs, the newest fighter in the Air Force. I chose the F-4C. This led me a few years later into taking up residence in Hanoi. I would end up staying in four different prisons during my 75 month Vietnam imprisonment, including time in the infamous Hanoi Hilton.[11] After attending combat survival school at Stead AFB, Nevada, I was assigned to MacDill AFB, Florida where I checked out in the F-4C.

F-4C Phantom[12]

I was now combat-ready. I was in the squadron that flew the first F-4C Phantoms from Florida across the Pacific ocean to Thailand. While on temporary duty in Thailand, I served a four month tour, during which I flew 59 combat missions over Laos and North Vietnam. Before my combat came to an abrupt end on December 2, 1966, I would end up flying 175 ½ combat missions.

My Thailand days were rewarding and life was good. In fact, it was one of the happiest, most satisfying times of my life. Against all odds, I had accomplished my lifelong dream and was now actually a fighter pilot. I was definitely on an upward trajectory, and was looking forward to a bright and promising future. But of course, things don't always go as planned.

"We can make our plans, but the LORD determines our steps."
Proverbs 16:9 (NLT)

"Eject!"

Chapter 3

"What's the difference between God and fighter pilots?
God doesn't think he's a fighter pilot." Anonymous

"It is generally inadvisable to eject directly over the area you just
bombed." USAF Manual

"It had all happened so fast; so unexpectedly. It seemed we were on another routine mission, when all of a sudden there was an explosion behind and under the aircraft, and faster than I can tell you both engine firelights started flashing and the entire warning light panel lit up like a Christmas tree.

"'We're hit! Eject!' I yelled to Mike Lane, my backseat co-pilot.[1] Training kicked in immediately. There was no time to waste. The plane was already out of control and beginning to fishtail. In vain, I moved the stick around, instantly realizing I had no stick authority, no more control of the airplane at all. That was it. This plane was going down. Mike didn't respond, so I pulled my handle, and was ejected out of the F-4 Phantom like a cork out of a champagne bottle.

"Getting shot down is just the most dramatic change of state that you can imagine. One minute you're a hot shot fighter pilot, Master of the Universe, and seconds later you're like a silk-stringed sky puppet, hanging helplessly from a parachute. It's a sudden and shocking transition.

"For Mike, my back seat co-pilot, the situation was no less dramatic. Having just transferred from the UK, it was his first mission up North. We'd been flying at 24,000 feet, going about 500 knots (approximately 575 mph), when all of a sudden, without warning, we felt a 'thump' and suddenly the plane was going out of control. Everything seemed to happen at once; very chaotic and confusing at first. Mike heard me yelling something, but couldn't quite make it out. It sounded like, 'Oh shit, something...' Then he felt the blast of wind in his face, as my canopy popped off when I ejected. Although I was still strapped to my seat, my seat was no longer in the plane! Mike suddenly found himself the aircraft commander, but only for a couple of seconds. It was time to get out of there! He pulled the ejection handle, and was also ejected from the airplane. Now we began our long descent into enemy territory."

Fortunately, they were able to get out of the plane in time. But the world they were now entering would prove to be hostile in the extreme. Ken continues: "As soon as I got out of the airplane, and opened my eyes, I saw the Phantom blow up ahead of me, so it was really close. Then I looked down between my feet, still in my ejection seat, and to my horror, saw another SAM (Surface-to-Air Missile) explode directly below me. What happened in the subsequent few seconds was even more exciting than the previous moments and is the single event in my life in which the hand of God was the most evident."

Artist representation of Captain Cordier's shoot down. Here the plane has already been hit once, and is going out of control. The second SAM has just exploded. Captain Cordier is in the first parachute (right center), while his co-pilot has just ejected from the cockpit (to the left, just over the airplane. The aircraft canopy can be seen lower middle of picture).

"They had fired two SAMs at us (Soviet tactics at the time were to fire SAMs in salvoes of two). The second one blew up right below me, and there was a big red, orange and black fireball growing; looking like the gates of hell. I couldn't believe I was headed right for it. I just had enough time to close my eyes and hold my breath before I felt this hot flash as I fell through the fireball. Amazingly, I didn't get a scratch. Not even a John Kerry splinter in my arm.

"Our lives would never be the same. In the blink of an eye, I went from 'favored son' of the USAF, to years in cruel and unforgiving primitive prisons. Like Job of the Bible, I would lose everything: freedom, family, friends and possessions." In such circumstances you have nothing left but faith in God; whether you sense it, think about it, acknowledge it or not."

A Biblical analogy can be drawn here from Joseph of the Bible[3]. He was stripped of his special apparel[4], tossed into a pit, then taken far away and imprisoned. Like Joseph, Ken would eventually come to an amazing redemption as well. But at this point, redemption would have been the last thing on his mind.

The Biblical analogies in this part of Ken's story are rich. In fact, God's fingerprints are all over it. Barbie, his wife, agrees. Speaking of his shoot down, she says, "When Ken speaks about his experiences, he comes right out and says 'The hand of God was around me.' And I know that's true, because he was shot out of the sky and watched his F-4 blow up. His back seater also got out. Now that's a God thing too. What timing! Then to come through that fireball!"

The days leading up to Ken's fateful encounter seemed perfectly normal. He'd grown accustomed to his life as a fighter pilot in Vietnam. He was good at it. "I was at the top of my game as a fighter pilot; in fact, I had a considerable dose of that sometimes fatal affliction which affects many combat pilots: complacency. I had flown a total of 175 missions over North and South Vietnam and Laos, and had been shot at many times. By this time, I felt invulnerable, because I had never received serious battle damage. Being shot at was very exciting, but I didn't regard it as a threat to my survival."

On the day before his last flight, Captain Cordier flew two 'counters', and he was happy about that. 'Counters' were so named because they counted towards the 100 missions required to get credit for a Vietnam tour. In order to count, it had to be over North Vietnam. He was getting close now. These last two counters brought his tally to 90. "Although I was scheduled to return to the States on December 14th, regardless of the number of missions flown, I was keen to leave Cam Ranh Bay with a completed tour on my record. To this day my ops officer, then Maj. Tim Boddie, remembers how I pestered him to schedule me for counters at least once a day, and how he felt guilty for scheduling me for my last fateful mission.

"It was late in the afternoon of December 1st, when I returned from my second mission of the day. I was tired after two long flights, so I decided to skip going back to the hooch for a shower and clean flight suit as I usually did, and elected instead to go straight to the Officers' Club for a couple of drinks and dinner. Although served at the O'Club, the food was the same as at the G.I. mess hall, and not held in high regard by the pilots. The bar was a good deal, however, as all drinks were 25 cents per shot, so we drank all the best brands, my poison of choice being JD Black.

I had no sooner walked into the bar after checking my gun and holster western-style in the bank of cubbyholes at the entrance (similar to saloons in the Old West—there was a 'no gun' policy in the club), when one of my squadron mates notified me that Ops wanted to see me. I was afraid he was going to take me off the B-66 escort mission I was scheduled for the next day, but he only wanted to catch me before I started drinking because he needed me to pull night strip alert. This meant spending the night in a trailer at the end of the runway, fully dressed, including boots and parachute harness. The bunks weren't very comfortable; they were old-fashioned military four inch thick cotton mats on top of horizontal stretched springs. Little did I know that in a matter of hours, I would have considered that bed an exquisite luxury.

35

"As luck would have it, I didn't get scrambled that night, so I got to sleep until relieved by the day shift the next morning. The most exciting night scrambles began just before daylight. The claxon horn would screech and you'd hit the deck running and be out the door before you were fully awake; run to the bird and rendezvous with your crew chief, who had been sleeping in the next trailer; scramble up the ladder and jump into the Martin Baker ejection seat, hitting the cartridge switch to spin up engine #1; fasten the seat belt and hook up the intercom while the crew chief clipped the shoulder harness and pulled the ejection seat safety pins. He would then hop back on the left engine intake to help the back-seater with the same pins and connectors while I started engine #2.

"The urgency to launch quickly was driven by the need to get ordnance on targets which may move at dawn. The FACs (the Forward Air Controllers)[5] would cruise around in the pre-dawn, looking for a wisp of smoke coming up through the dense jungle foliage. Our job was to deliver the napalm and help cook the VC breakfast before they packed up and dispersed into the jungle. Number 2 (i.e. the second plane assigned to this mission) would join up after takeoff and we would check in with 'Red Crown', the ATC (Air Traffic Control) radar ship, for a handoff to the waiting FAC. It was always very gratifying to work with a FAC who had enemy sighted, knowing you would likely ruin some VC's (Việt Cộng)[6] day.

"When the morning crew showed up to relieve us, I dropped in at squadron ops (i.e. squadron headquarters) to be briefed for the big mission up north. This one was very sought after by the squadron jocks because it was our only chance to ever get a shot at a MiG[7]— every fighter pilot's dream. We never got to the briefing because "Stormy", the weather officer, was there to tell us the entire strike force mission was on a weather hold due to cloud cover over the target areas. This didn't affect us directly because our mission was to protect the EB-66 whose mission was to monitor the enemy's radar emissions (the ECM-Electronic CounterMeasures[8]) and communications while the strike force flew in and out from the target."

EB-66 - Electronic Warfare Bomber

Unfortunately, no one told Captain Cordier that this EB-66 was not carrying the jamming equipment designed to black out the SAM radars. "Had I known this I would have devoted more time to watching what was going on below. I would then very likely have seen the SAM, looking like a flaming telegraph pole, coming up at me. Had I seen it, I might have been able to avoid it through evasive maneuvering.

"Until the weather cleared, the strike force was on hold and so were we. That meant going to the Club for breakfast—scrambled reconstituted eggs, SOS and no coffee—that causes indigestion! After breakfast I went back to the hooch for some shut-eye, as the weather hold could go on all day. This was to be the last sleep I would get for the next 40 or so hours which would encompass the singular most dramatic event of my life."

For Captain Cordier, this should have been a very good day. First of all, he might possibly get a shot at a MIG. Secondly, this mission would be a 'counter', Number 91 over North Vietnam, and ever closer to the magic number of 100 missions.

Meanwhile, low clouds and steady rain continued. There was a problem with one of the other plane's "inertial nav" (a navigation aid)[9]. It had to be dropped from the mission, leaving only the flight lead and Capt. Cordier's fighter to provide cover for the EB-66. It was fueled up and armed with mission-appropriate weapons: four AIM-9 Side Winders (heat seeking missiles) and four AIM-7 Sparrows (radar guided missiles).

F-4 Phantom cockpit

Finally, they got the order to launch, and launch they did, but the mission would never be completed. Instead, Ken and his backseat co-pilot Mike Lane would keep an unwanted appointment with a Soviet SAM.[10] From the moment of initial contact, Ken knew their plane had been struck by a SAM. These things were deadly, and were taking their toll on American planes and pilots.[11] On December 2, 1966, Ken and Mike became the next on the list.

"The extent of my 'luck' can be seen when the kill mechanism of a Soviet SA-II missile is explained. When the warhead detonates, the cylindrical metal casing breaks up into metal fragments which fly out in an expanding doughnut-shaped ring of shrapnel. If one is within its lethal radius, hits are virtually assured. 'Chance' put me on exactly the correct flight path to fall through the hole of that 'doughnut', and live to tell the tale."

As Ken's wife Barbie said, "What timing! How is it that he would fall just right, at the right speed, angle and flight path to have a second SAM explode right under him, and then to come right through the center of that fireball, with the expanding ring of fire, and not get a scratch? Is that all coincidence? No. Not coincidence. A God-incidence."[11]

"When you pass through the waters, I will be with you; and when you pass through the rivers, they will not sweep over you. When you walk through the fire, you will not be burned; the flames will not set you ablaze." Isaiah 43:2

"This miraculous escape from the two SAMs convinced me that there was something else in store for me, something in the grand scheme of things which I had yet to do; otherwise my story should have ended on December 2, 1966."

After miraculously passing through this fireball, Ken opened his eyes and took in his circumstances. "I still had a long ways to go, but I panicked for the first time in my life. I had this gripping feeling that if I didn't get out of that seat I'd ride it into the ground. My reasoning was that the flames, the heat from the fireball, had burned away the automatic parachute extraction device and it wouldn't work. So against everything I'd been trained to do, I pulled the handles, cut the lap belt and the leg restraints, pushed away from the seat, grabbed the D-ring, pulled the handle, and

BAM— the parachute opened. I couldn't wait to see silk above me, but again that was against what I'd been trained to do. You're supposed to wait until you get to a lower altitude before you deploy the parachute because of the opening shock."

A manned parachute drops approximately 1,000 feet a minute. Ken was at 24,000 feet when he was hit. As he now says, "I had a few minutes left in the descent. I assessed the situation, and I couldn't tell where I was because there was an under-cast. Eventually I fell through that, and if it hadn't been such a tense moment, I think I would have enjoyed this because it was like floating down into a sea of cotton candy, very quiet and serene in this layer of clouds. Then I fell though the cloud deck, and I looked down and I couldn't believe it. All these missions that I'd flown over Vietnam were mostly over jungle. But there wasn't any jungle. It was all rice paddies and hamlets, and no place to hide. So, I knew I had a very slim chance, if any, of evading.

I finally hit the ground and got out of my parachute. The first thing I sensed was that I reeked of gunpowder. So I wasn't hallucinating about the fireball, and my eyebrows, I saw later, were singed off, and I had freckled powder burns on my arms and forehead. Then I looked around and saw a group of peasants running across the rice paddies yelling with a couple of them waving rifles. Several weeks before, I had watched the movie 'The Bridges at Toko-Ri'. In the closing scene, William Holden was on the ground, having just been shot down. He elected to shoot it out with the enemy running to capture him. He was hit and the screen went black.

That scene flashed through my mind, and I knew I wasn't going home that night to my Beverly Hills mansion, so I did the sensible thing and threw my 38 revolver as far as I could and stood up and held up my hands. I was quickly captured, as was Mike, and they marched us off to their village, where they held us until the army came with a truck. Then the rough stuff began. They stripped us to our jockey shorts, blindfolded us, tied our hands behind us, and threw us in the back of a truck where they tied us to the side, and off we went to Hanoi."

Ken's situation would get much worse; but the Lord watches over His own.

Captured American pilot (identity unknown)

*"The L*ORD *watches over you... (He) will watch over your coming and going, both now and forevermore."* Psalm 121:5, 8

The Breaking Point

Chapter 4

*"Isn't it great to be alive and free! I was imprisoned by the
North Vietnamese communists for 6 years and 3 months under
really harsh and sometimes unbelievable conditions. You might
think that I lost my life and freedom during that time. But I didn't.
As long as you have freedom in your mind,
you have a degree of freedom."*
Colonel Ken Cordier[1]

*"You can chain me, you can torture me, you can even destroy this
body, but you will never imprison my mind."*
Mahatma Gandhi[2]

*"Do not be afraid of those who kill the body
but cannot kill the soul."* Matthew 10:28

Here in America, we can say anything we want. After all, it's
a free country. Right?

Well, yes, but some words are more sensitive than others;
more demanding of respect. For example the word "torture".
We're not talking about political correctness here.

Here's an example: according to Maj. Gen. George Fay's
investigation, inmates at Abu Ghraib were "tortured" by being
forced "to wear women's underwear, sometimes on their heads."[3]
Tortured? Really? After learning a little about what our Vietnam
POWs went through, one might cringe when the term 'torture' is
used in a less than accurate fashion.

Merriam-Webster defines torture as: "the act of causing severe physical pain as a form of punishment or as a way to force someone to do or say something."[4] Colonel Cordier puts it this way: "Real torture usually involves permanent mental or physical damage. Interrogation techniques which cause temporary discomfort, however distressing, are correctly labeled as 'enhanced interrogation techniques.'"

Once tied and thrown in the back of the truck, Ken and his back seat pilot were off to Hanoi. "We stopped at every village along the way. It was the same scene everywhere: they'd roll the canvas sides of the truck up and you'd hear angry voices gathering. They threw stones at us and whacked us with bamboo sticks, but the worst part of it was that they all wanted to spit on us. By the time we got to Hanoi we were covered with spit, and we didn't get a chance to bathe for several days.

"The ride to Hanoi was really painful. I was sitting on a plank, and the roads were terrible. Every time we'd hit a chuckhole, I'd bounce up in the air, land on my tailbone, and would just be screaming in agony. I felt like my back was broken and, indeed, I later found out that it was.

"We finally got to Hanoi the next morning, arriving at what I would later learn was the "Hanoi Hilton" prison. Mike and I were separated, and I was immediately put into a room. I couldn't see, of course, so all I know is that they made me sit on the floor, blindfolded, with my hands still tied behind my back. Presently a man entered the room and started asking questions in English. At first it was name, rank, service number, date of birth, those questions that we were obliged to answer under the Geneva Conventions. Then he moved quickly past that and started asking military questions.

"'What kind of airplane were you flying?' he asked. They assumed I was up there bombing. I politely refused to answer that question.

"'What were your targets?' Same response.

After a while he feigned anger and said, 'You must answer our questions! What makes you think you don't have to answer my questions?'

"Well, your country signed the Geneva Conventions on treatment of POWs," I said evenly.

"'Nonsense! You are not a POW. You're a war criminal. The US did not declare war on us, so you are all here illegally, and we're going to treat you as criminals. If you don't answer my questions, you will be severely punished.'

"I thought, 'Yeah, right. I've heard this before. It's probably like Hogan's' Heroes. They'll put me in the cooler for a month.'

"Well, that wasn't the case. They untied my hands and put them in manacles (clamps) behind my back, put ropes around my upper arms, shoved me to the floor with a foot on my back and cinched up on my arms until my elbows touched behind me. Then they just went away and left me.

"Now this was real torture. With my back hurting to begin with, I don't think I withstood it for more than an hour. After I yelled long enough and loud enough, they came in and loosened the ropes and resumed the interrogation. This time they removed the blindfold, and here were three little Vietnamese guys with 'beanie' hats sporting the red star looking very serious.

"'If you refuse to cooperate you will be severely punished.'

"I figured I'm going to have to tell them something because I can't take this painful torture. So I started making up answers as I went along. However, he was astute enough to realize that I was just putting him on.

Standing up, he said, 'I don't have time for this. You're wasting my time, so you'll be punished more.'

"At this point, I was still feeling pretty brave, so I said, 'This is barbaric. You're torturing me, when I need to see a doctor.'

Looking mildly puzzled, he replied, 'You're not bleeding. What's wrong?'

"'I think my back is broken; I'm in a lot of pain.' Well, that was a big mistake. Later, when I was in contact with other POWs, I found out that if a man was injured, they tortured the injury to make him break sooner. This time when they put me back in the ropes, and had me on the floor, they put another rope around my neck and ankles, and arched me backwards as far as they could. That gave new meaning to the word pain. Here I was hog-tied, and in the ropes again and I didn't last long that time. The pain was so excruciating I tried hitting my head on the floor to knock myself out to get relief, but all I did was make my head hurt. I screamed, 'Alright, I'll answer your questions.'

"So they loosened the ropes and resumed the interrogation. I noticed they were taking a lot of notes of everything I said, so I decided I'd better figure out some way to keep track of my story and stick to it. I decided I'd tell them the truth, but multiply everything by three. I didn't think that that would work very long. Surely they'd realize how absurd it was to make these outrageous claims of the range of our radar and other weapon systems capabilities.

"I tried it and it worked. It was easy enough when they'd double back and repeat a question. I'd just answer truthfully and multiply by three. That got me though that interrogation. I spent the rest of that day and the next day with periodic interrogations, mostly the same questions. But also some political questions:

Interrogator: "What do you think about the war?"

Captain Cordier: "I think about the war."

Interrogator: "Do you support your government?"

Captain Cordier: "Yes, I do."

Captain Cordier continued, "They were looking for me to make some anti-war statement or say that I thought it was wrong for the U.S. to be in Vietnam, which I never did. I never suffered for telling my true feelings. According to several former POWs[5], the aim of the torture was often not so much acquiring military information, as it was to acquire material for propaganda. It was ultimately to break the will of the prisoners, both individually and as a group. Their goal was to get written or recorded statements from the prisoners which criticized U.S. conduct of the war and praised how the North Vietnamese treated them well. Such POW statements would be viewed as a propaganda victory in the battle to sway world and U.S. domestic opinion against the U.S. war effort.

After three days of intense interrogations, his 'confession' (only four little paragraphs) was typed up, and brought to him, along with the ropes and cuffs. "The Rabbit" [2], chief NV political officer for all the POW camps, slammed them on the table and said, 'Now you will write your war crimes confession.'

"'I can't do that.' I answered. 'I haven't committed crimes and I can't confess to crimes I haven't committed.' So he had the guard tie me up. I couldn't take this torture again, so I said, 'OK, I'll write it.' I then had to copy it in my own handwriting, and sign it, which I did. I broke. I gave in. And that's against my personal code of conduct: 'Never give up. Never give in.' But I gave in. It was a horrible feeling."

"The first paragraph stated that I had violated Vietnamese airspace and committed crimes against the Vietnamese people, bombing villages and killing innocent women and children. In the second paragraph I condemned my government for the illegal, immoral and unjust war and demanded that U.S. withdraw from Vietnam and allow the Vietnamese people to settle their own affairs. The third paragraph asked the Vietnamese people to forgive me of my crimes.

"It was just galling to copy this confession. The worst part was at the very end where I thanked the Vietnamese people for their lenient and humane treatment, and signed it.

~~~~~~~~~~~~~

Torture is effective. [6] Anyone who has experienced true torture would attest that everyone has their breaking point. When Col. Cordier speaks of "giving in", one could argue that that is not the best way to express it. Instead, how about: he submitted under extreme duress.

Early on, when interrogations were prominent in his daily routine, Captain Cordier realized that the Viet Cong were more interested in screening the prisoners to identify who might be vulnerable to exploitation for useful propaganda, than they were about obtaining actual military information. After all, military intelligence becomes stale after a few days or a couple of weeks at most.

In the end, North Vietnamese torture was sufficiently brutal and prolonged that "virtually every American POW" [7] eventually submitted to their captors' demands, to one degree or another. Some gave more, some gave less, but all gave. After finally being forced to make anti-American statements, Senator John McCain later wrote, "I had learned what we all learned over there: Every man has his breaking point. I had reached mine."[8]

Realizing this, the Americans' aim became to absorb as much torture as they could before giving in.[9] One later described an internal POW code, developed and instructed to the new arrivals as: "Take physical torture until you are right at the edge of losing your ability to be rational. At that point, lie, do, or say whatever you must do to survive. But you first must take physical torture." [10]

After making statements, the POWs would admit to each other what they had done, lest shame or guilt consume them or make them more vulnerable to additional North Vietnamese pressure.[11]

Nevertheless, the POWs obsessed over what they had done, and years after their release would still be haunted by 'confessions' or other statements they had made. As another POW later said, "To this day I get angry with myself. But we did the best we could. We realized over time that we all fall short of what we aspire to be. That is where forgiveness comes in." [14]

"If we confess our sins, he is faithful and just and will forgive us our sin and purify us from all unrighteousness."
1 John 1:9

Although North Vietnam issued denials, U.S. military officials were convinced that our people were being tortured. This was not confirmed however, until May 17, 1966, when Cmdr. Jeremiah Denton Jr. gave clear confirmation during his ingenious 'eye-blinking interview', broadcast throughout the United States.[12] Ten months into his confinement as one of the highest-ranking officers to be taken prisoner in Vietnam, Denton was forced by his captors to participate in a 1966 televised propaganda interview, broadcast in the United States.

On May 17, 1966, while answering questions and feigning trouble with the blinding television lights, Denton blinked his eyes in Morse code, spelling the word "TORTURE" over and over, confirming for the first time to the U.S. Office of Naval Intelligence that American POWs were in fact being tortured. Yes, our POWs were being subjected to abuse, malnutrition and extreme torture; including rope bindings, irons, beatings, and prolonged solitary confinement. The worst years of this mistreatment began in 1966 before Captain Cordier's arrival at the Zoo in December 1966.

Solitary Man

Chapter 5

"I'll be what I am,
A solitary man,
Solitary man."
Neil Diamond 1966 [1]

It was indeed a dichotomy of epic proportions. Mere hours before, Captain Cordier was at the top of his game as a seasoned fighter pilot with lots of combat experience and perhaps a bit too much self-confidence. Now here he was in the infamous "Hanoi Hilton": abused, tortured and assured of more of the same.

The "Hanoi Hilton" was a sarcastic nickname for the Hỏa Lò Prison. Built by the French for Vietnamese criminals and political prisoners during their occupation of Vietnam (1887-1954), it was later used by the Vietnamese Army during the war to house, interrogate and torture captured servicemen, mostly American pilots who had been shot down. It was a triangular array of buildings the size of a city block, surrounded by a dry moat and twenty-foot walls studded with sharp hunks of glass and topped with electrified barbed wire. The name Hỏa Lò, is commonly translated as "fiery furnace" or even "Hell's hole".

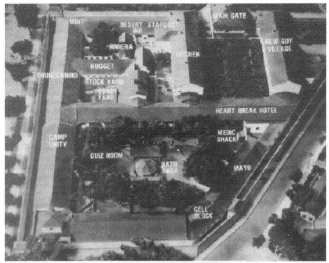

The 'Hanoi Hilton' of 1970

Captain Cordier would spend three days there for his initial interrogations before being transferred to "the Zoo", the main POW camp located in the southwestern suburbs of Hanoi.

The afternoon of the third day, after he had completed his war crimes confession, Capt. Cordier was taken to New Guy Village courtyard. This was a section of the Hanoi Hilton made up of cells to receive the American prisoners. It was usually the first stop for all the American pilots captured after being shot down.

A typical cell was 8 feet by 9 feet, and consisted of two solid concrete beds, with metal and wood stocks at the foot of each. The concrete bunks were about 3 ½ feet high and 2 ½ feet apart. The door had a small peephole and was flanked by windows which had been covered over by a thin layer of concrete. Sanitation was poor. Cells were infested with insects and rodents. The food, by normal standards, was not fit to eat. Medical treatment was poor to nonexistent and was provided only when a captive's condition became serious, or the captive became cooperative.

There, he was led to a small bamboo enclosure where there was a water tap. The guard gave him a small thin towel and a piece of lye soap and pointing to the water tap barked, "Wat!"

"Even though the water was very cold, I was glad for the chance to scrub off the spit and dirt. I went at it and took the first of many cold baths over the coming 2,282 days. This was my first chance to look around, but I wasn't able to make much of my surroundings. The walls were stained and peeling yellow ochre and the shuttered windows were painted a faded mossy green. I could see a stretch of outside wall with several strands of barbed wire over the top which had pieces of broken glass sticking up.

"Next, through gestures, he led me towards the next building to empty my rusty bucket, which served as a toilet. I caught movement out of the corner of my eye, and thought I saw a grey cat running along the base of the wall, but a second glance confirmed that it was the biggest rat that I had ever seen. About then the guard returned and yelled at me, motioning to move towards the "Heartbreak" cellblock. "Heartbreak Hotel" was the name we gave to the block of five solitary cells primarily used to hold prisoners during the initial interrogations phase.

"Back to the stinking little cell!!! I sat on the narrow concrete ledge, looked at the rusty leg irons and wondered if they were still used. I didn't have long to wait until the guard returned with a blanket, mosquito net, two pair of dark blue drawstring boxer shorts, two tee shirts, a cotton turtleneck sweatshirt, a pair of striped pajamas, a pair of rubber tire sandals, and a green enamel tin cup decorated with Korean and Vietnamese writing. This was my personal equipment issue, and I didn't even have to sign a hand receipt. Little did I realize that I would be there long enough to wear out these clothing items."

Capt. Cordier's first three days of captivity were now drawing to a close. He'd been introduced to the North Vietnamese up close and personal. The mistreatment and torture would continue once he was at the Zoo, but he now had an idea of what he was in for.

"They put me in a cell in 'Heartbreak' and left me alone for the rest of the evening.

"Next, they came around and blindfolded me and led me out to a truck, and off we went to the main camp we called 'The Zoo'. I was put into a solitary cell. That means there was no one to talk to, no way to communicate so I was really feeling low. I wasn't prepared for what had happened to me the last three days—I could hardly get my mind around it and begin to make the adjustment to my fall from grace." Perhaps it was best that he couldn't take it all in at once, as it was just too much to absorb in large doses.

"No test or temptation that comes your way is beyond the course of what others have had to face. All you need to remember is that God will never let you down; he'll never let you be pushed past your limit; he'll always be there to help you come through it."
1 Corinthians 10:13 The Message (MSG)

"I was fortunate to only be in solitary confinement for 1 month," Ken now says[3]. How true. Solitary is no small thing. The longer you are in it, the more consequences you are likely to pay.[4]

Ken continues, "Not long after I was locked in this solitary cell, someone started tapping on the wall. It wasn't Morse code, and it made no sense. When I was in the interrogation room at New Guy Village, I was left alone for a few minutes, and got a look at a matrix code scratched into the side of the table, but I didn't have the time to study it, and got it all wrong.

"This attempt to establish communication was cut off by the shattering sound of wrench on shell casing, which signaled it was 9pm and time to commit my painful bones to the 'rack' (my name for the planks which were my bed)."

Soon enough however, Ken would learn this POW 'tap' code. It would be a lifeline for all the prisoners there. It was a simple matrix coDE,

TAPS	1	2	3	4	5
1	A	B	C	D	E
2	F	G	H	I	J
3	L	M	N	O	P
4	Q	R	S	T	U
5	V	W	X	Y	Z

Tap Code Chart

Ken explains, "It worked like this. First, you would memorize the tap code chart. Once you knew the chart, you were ready to communicate. Each letter is communicated by tapping two numbers: the first designating the row; the second designating the column. For example, to specify the letter 'B', one taps once, pauses, and then taps twice. Because of the difficulty and length of time required for specifying a single letter, prisoners often devised abbreviations and acronyms for common items or phrases, such as 'GN' for Good Night, or 'GBU' for God Bless You.

"Notice the critical absence of the letter "K". Since our alphabet has 26 characters, one has to be omitted to make the 5 X 5 matrix work. I thought it obvious (and still do) to drop the letter Z, and that is how I memorized it. Consequently, everything after the letter K was one character off, making no sense when I tried to decipher the message.

"We were innovators in abbreviations to save tapping, similar to texting shorthand used today. The only thing we didn't have that they have today is LOL. It would have been neat to have it to show appreciation for a funny joke.

"As things progressed, we learned everybody's names and what the current interrogation topics were. We also shared background information, like, 'Are you married?' 'Kids?'

'Family?' 'Where do you like to vacation?' 'Where have you been stationed?' With endless days of nothing to do (except to keep from getting caught tapping), we resorted to telling jokes, that is, tapping jokes on the wall.

"Now when I tell you a joke and you think it's funny, you laugh. That makes me feel good; I entertained you. If you think it's a bad joke, you give me a Bronx cheer or roll your eyes. The way we signified laughing was with our nails, clicking on the walls. If it was considered a bad joke, we'd thump the wall with our elbow."

After a month of solitary life, an unexpected ray of sunshine appeared. During an interrogation, Capt. Cordier was asked, "Would you like to have a roommate?"

"Yes, that would be nice."

"You must promise to obey the camp regulations. That is, no talking out loud, no singing or whistling, no exercising, and definitely no communication with other POWs."

"I said, 'OK.'" Then in walked Mike Lane, Ken's back-seater! They were then marched off to a two-man cell in a different building, where they would take up residence together."

"For the Lord hears the needy
and does not despise
his own people who are prisoners."
Psalm 69:3

Interrogators, Tormentors, and other Prison Staff

Chapter 6

"The trick to surviving an interrogation is patience. Don't offer up anything. Don't explain. Answer the question and only the question that is asked so you don't accidentally put your neck in a noose." Lauri Halse Anderson [1]

The interrogators were hated by all the POWs. They held the keys to abuse, beatings, solitary confinement and tortures of all kinds. 'The Elf' would go to torture as quickly as any of the other interrogators to accomplish his goals. His nick name seemed to fit him well. Small and skinny, with badly yellowed teeth and receding gums, but he had no problem getting his point across—nor his questions.

The Rabbit

Most of the prison staff had been given nicknames by their detainees. This was especially true for their chief tormentors: the interrogators. A few examples of these included: Magoo, AB (for After Birth), Frenchie, Rabbit (because of his big ears), Smiley, Ichabod (who was tall and skinny), Spot (due to the birthmark on his cheek), and the Bug (for his wild Bug eyes).

Compared with some of the others, the Elf was considered one of the better officers to have a 'quiz' with. He was willing to allow the prisoners to change the subject at times. He'd told some of them that he'd been a math teacher before the army, and he'd even been known to talk a little about his family.

He was a chain smoker, and that worked to the POW's advantage, as he could be generous with his cigarettes during interrogations. But make no mistake, the Elf was in charge. He was Captain Cordier's principal interrogator while he was at 'The Zoo'. He'd see him often, especially at the beginning of his imprisonment.

"NNIYH?" For the Elf, although probably done unconsciously (like people today saying "you know"), it was just a way to punctuate his sentences, often accompanied with the nodding of his head in little jerks. It was a funny little mannerism, all his own. It would have been comical if not for the serious nature of the situation, but no one was laughing to his face.

Ken remembers, "My biggest mistake during my initial interrogations was to try to debate the merits of Democracy versus Communism or to try to make points. Elf had the hammer and if I ever did score a point, he surely wasn't going to concede it. Instead, the only indicator that I had made a point was that he got very angry, and after a screaming tongue-lashing would send me back to my cell to 'think about my crimes'.

"On a number of occasions we were punished by either kneeling with arms stretched out above our heads or standing with arms straight up, hands against the wall, until the evening gong. If you were lucky enough to have a cellmate(s), they would lay on the floor with an eye to the crack under the door, watching for guards, sometimes for hours on end. If you don't think this is a big deal, try kneeling on your kitchen tile floor with arms extended over your head and stay that way for even five minutes.

"Interrogations were my principle distraction during the early days. I dreaded them, because they were scheduled in one hour blocks, which included time to march the previous prisoner to his cell and bring out the next. This meant no less than 50 minutes on the little stool which got to be very painful after about 15 minutes. I would hold my hands at my sides and occasionally try to push down on the edge of the stool to relieve my back. The Elf took this as a gesture of defiance and ordered me to sit politely with my hands in my lap. When I protested about my back pain, he ordered me to keep silent." Posture reflected attitude. Poor posture reflected a bad attitude, and a bad attitude wouldn't be tolerated.

Interrogations didn't always follow a 9-to-5 schedule. "As bad as the daytime interrogations were, night interrogations were much worse. The guards would suddenly open the door with a lot of noise, yell at me to get dressed in the long striped pajamas and march me to the 'quiz shack' located across camp, punctuated by extra pushing and shoving. This is a very effective interrogation technique because you are somewhat disoriented by being awakened from a sound asleep, and fearful that something bad is going to happen; otherwise, why not wait until the next day? Additionally, the interrogator was usually in an ugly mood because he had pulled the night shift and was in no mood for resistance games.

"To survive a POW situation, or any major challenge in life, preparation is key. While there's no way to prepare specifically to be a POW, the training I received in survival school did give me something to fall back on when I found myself in the real life situation. For example, during the resistance training phase of combat survival school, the instructor played the part of an interrogator. He lectured me with a lot of communist propaganda which was boring and lacking in believable ideas. At this point of the training I was sleep deprived, but trying to 'play the game'. However, I gave away my feelings when I unconsciously smirked. The instructor stopped right there and said, 'Never smirk! If you smirk, that's an insult to them and it'll go very badly for you.' So when I found myself in the real life situation, exhausted, feeling giddy, and wanting to laugh, I remembered my training, and bit my cheeks until they bled to keep from laughing."

"Those who guard their mouths and their tongues keep themselves from calamity."
Proverbs 21:23

Prison Daze

Chapter 7

*"Suffering is part of the human condition, and it comes to us all.
The key is how we react to it, either turning away from
God in anger and bitterness or growing
closer to Him in trust and confidence."*
Billy Graham[1]

"I feel monotony and death to be almost the same."
Charlotte Bronte (1816-1855) [2]

"We got to get out of this place, if it's the last thing we ever do."
Song performed by The Animals, 1965 [3]

Monotony preys on itself. As the days became weeks, and the weeks months, monotony inevitably settled in. It's a soul killer, and would play an increasingly large role as time went on. Although interrogations continued, the flow of useful material from the POWs soon began to ebb. They had wrung out all the useful military intelligence from each new prisoner in a couple of days. In the long term, as covered previously, propaganda took on more importance and that was the basis for the endless interrogations which the men endured for several years.

With the passage of time, they began to fall into a routine. Like a bad repeating dream, it always started the same way.

Captain Cordier easily recalls the daily routine he'd soon learn: "I can describe it with 'B's: Be no talking. Be no reading. Be no writing. Be no exercising. It constituted a very harsh regimen of confinement. A typical day began at 5am, when they rang the gong. The gong wasn't a round brass gong that they hit with a mallet. It was an empty 85mm shell casing hung from a tree, and the guard would beat on it with a wrench. It made a horrible noise and got you awake in a hurry. By this time my back was really hurting, and I was ready to get up anyway.

So we got up, and the first thing was to fold up the mosquito net. They gave us all a mosquito net, which was the one humane thing they did. The place was humming with mosquitos. It would have been terrible as well as unhealthy to have to deal with the mosquitoes at night. As it was, we went around with bites all over anyway. So I untied the two corners of the mosquito net, and let it hang down against the wall. I was later informed by the turn-key that this was not acceptable. He made a 'roll-up' motion and I figured that I should fold it up neatly and do the same with my blanket—a typical GI procedure in any army. He emphasized the point by whacking me on the head with his key ring—a gesture I was to become familiar with over the coming months.

Next we were supposed to sit on our beds and 'think about our war crimes!' It was all part of the enemy's mantra "You're not prisoners of war, you're criminals". For those having problems admitting their war crimes, Hanoi Hannah and the interrogators were ever-present to remind them often and in detail. Little matter if it was true or not. After all, the goal of propaganda is not truth, but victory. Aeschylus, the Greek tragic dramatist, said many centuries ago, "Truth is the first casualty of war." [4] And so it is. Adolph Hitler, the master of 20th century evil and propaganda said: "Make the lie big, make it simple, keep saying it, and eventually they will believe it. "[5]

Ken continues, "At 6am the Voice of Vietnam came on. They used a lot of propaganda to try to make us homesick, but at the end of the 30 minute broadcast, they played two American popular songs. That was the highpoint of my day, a time to close my eyes and transport myself mentally to a far better time and an infinitely better place. My favorite song was Nancy Wilson singing "It's the Good Life." The tinkling cocktail piano music in the background conjured up some fond memories of pleasant hours in a piano bar in San Francisco on my way to Vietnam. Another favorite was Petula Clark singing *Downtown*. Going "downtown" was fighter pilot slang for missions over Hanoi. I'll never understand why they didn't just turn the radio off when they got to the music. They had the music at the end of the program to get the GIs to hang on and listen. So we'd get some current popular music, which was a big morale boost for us."

The *Voice of Vietnam* used several announcers, but the one best known by the POWs was certainly "Hanoi Hannah", a.k.a. "the Dragon Lady, a.k.a. "Thu Huong" (i.e. "the Fragrance of Autumn"). Few if any desertions are thought to have happened because of her propaganda work and the G.I.s hooted at her scare tactics.

'Hanoi Hannah', the 'Fragrance of Autumn'

~~~~~~~~~~~~

Breakfast of Champions

"After the Voice of Vietnam, we waited for the morning meal. That came around 10-11am, and consisted of a bowl of crudely milled brown rice and a bowl of soup. I don't mean Campbell's soup either. Think boiled vegetables. The vegetable depended on the time of year. In the summertime it was boiled greens, no meat, no seasoning. Imagine a cross between spinach and seaweed. The fall was the best. We'd get a couple chunks of squash. Winter was absolutely the worst. We got cabbage every day for four months.

"Basically, we were given a bare subsistence diet, so there was no waste or garbage, although the garbage thrown out of most American homes would have been a treat. Suffice it to say we were always hungry."

In late 1967, the prisons were filling up with downed pilots, so they opened a new addition to the Zoo which we called the Zoo Annex. This compound had four buildings, each with two 18 ft. by 21 ft. rooms, holding eight men in each room. In May 1968 a number of the POWs, including Ken were moved into the Annex. At first, this seemed like an improvement, having seven cellmates instead of one or two. However, the close confinement of being locked up 24/7 with no privacy and every conversation being heard and commented on by the other seven cellmates proved to be tiresome and tedious. Ken called it 'the sardine can syndrome.'

The eight man cells in the 'Zoo Annex' had a step-down behind the entry door such that three of us could sit on the floor with our feet in the well rather than cross-legged on the floor, as there were no beds or stools to sit on. One day, when the guard let us out to pick up our rice and soup bowls, he paused as always to take our bow, then locked the door. Everyone then sat down to devour their meager ration. I had set my two bowls on the floor prior to bowing, and when I sat down, I clumsily knocked over my soup bowl, spilling the contents on the floor. Applying the three second rule, I quickly swept the broth and few chucks of kohlrabi back into my bowl and proceeded to eat the remains of the soup. This was viewed with disdain by several of my cellmates, who let me know in no uncertain terms how disgusting it was to watch me eat off the dirty floor. I shot right back that it they would care to share their ration I would gladly throw my tainted soup in the toilet bucket. It came as no surprise that they declined my offer. It was interesting to note later that I suffered no gastrointestinal discomfort as a result of eating that 'dirty soup'.

"After the morning meal we were supposed to get out in a little court yard to bathe, ten minutes a day. The water source was a seepage well. We'd drop a bucket down and pull up muddy water to wash ourselves and our clothes. They gave us a cake of what looked like Grandma's lye soap every 60 days, and that was to wash our bodies, our clothes, and to shave (we were not permitted to have any facial hair) once a week using cold, sometimes muddy water, with a rusty razor blade made in communist Bulgaria. It was miserable. I called it institutional torture. Actually, we only got out 2 or 3 times a week, as the guards were lazy and preferred to hang out with their buddies and chain smoke cigarettes, as opposed to keeping an eye on us.

"Then at noon they rang the gong and we were allowed to take a siesta. That seemed like a good deal, to escape the miserable environment by sleeping for two hours. But not so fast —most of the guards took a siesta, too, so security was much reduced with fewer guards walking around. Therefore, instead of sleeping, we used the time to communicate using the tap code.

"One day some poor guy got caught tapping, and we found out what the consequences were. They hauled him out to interrogation, and demanded to know who he was tapping with.

"Of course the guy would deny everything, 'No, I wasn't trying to communicate with anybody. I was just practicing playing drums.'

"'No, you lie. If you don't tell us with who you were communicating with, you will be punished!'

"'No, it was nothing.'

"'You lie, you must tell us now or you will be severely punished (code for the ropes). Tell us now!'

"So they would put him in the ropes. Whenever they really wanted something from us, the default position was 'put him in the ropes.' They knew we would break. With a lot of mental anguish, the guy would admit, 'OK I was tapping with John Brodak next door.'

"Now they got what they wanted; on to the next link. What followed was predictable. They'd take Brodak out, torture him, find out who he was tapping with, and before it was over, they would learn that the whole camp was connected. This included not only the cells within a cell block, but the other buildings as well. We had many innovative ways to communicate between buildings. In the end, many men would be tortured before giving up the information demanded. We called it a 'comm purge.'

"It is said, every cloud has a silver lining. In this case the silver lining was a complete shuffle of the camp. My cell mate was taken across camp to another building, and someone came in with me, and so on. They had a master plan where they shuffled everybody all over the camp, believing that this would break up our organization and our ability to communicate.

Ironically, the scramble worked in our favor because it actually increased the flow of information. More importantly, it was a great morale boost to get a new roommate(s). Can you imagine being locked up 24/7 with one or two guys? It only took about a week or two to hear all his stories and tell all of yours. Then, it was back to boredom and monotony.

"As soon as the guard locked the door and walked away, I started tapping on the wall. 'Hi, I'm Ken Cordier. Who are you?' By the next day the whole camp was in contact again. They were never able to stop us from communicating in spite of the torture and beatings.

"Life went on like this, very harsh. I lost a lot of weight during the first 6-9 months due to the poor diet. We were forbidden to exercise. If you got caught exercising, it was a week in irons. That is, with your legs in irons tied to the foot of the board, and your hands in handcuffs behind you. They would come around twice a day to let you out of the handcuffs to eat your bowl of rice and use the bucket. If you didn't have a cellmate to help you use the bucket during the rest of the time, it got pretty nasty.

"This is how we lived during the early years. We just adapted as best we could. It was hard to stay optimistic. We tried to keep ourselves from losing hope by communicating.

"By this time, I was living in a new part of the prison, where we had eight men in a cell, in an 18 X 21 foot room. After many months of harsh prison life (we called it 'the grinder'), I became aware that we were becoming permanently 'down-at-the-mouth'. I remember thinking about the movie Papillion, and the scene where Steve McQueen stuck his head out of the inspection door to get his weekly shave and asking the guy in the next cell, 'How do I look?' The response was, 'Terrible.' This applied to us. We never had anything to smile about, much less laugh. I said, 'I have to do something about this.'"

That's when Ken instituted his smile exercises. "Every morning, when I did my exercises, I would do twenty repetitions of rock-up-on-my-tip-toes for ten seconds and hold a forced 'Ipana Toothpaste' grin. I thought this would tighten up my facial muscles so I wouldn't have the 'prison drawn' demeanor. I don't know if it really worked, but some of my cellmates joined me in the attempt while others scoffed, 'There's Cordier again, over there grinning like a Cheshire cat!'"

"A cheerful heart is good medicine."
Proverbs 17:22

A foreboding, pervasive monotony accompanied the frequent abuse; day after day, week after week, year after year. Ever-innovative, the POWs found ways to keep occupied. One important way was to memorize the names of all the POWs there.

Col. Cordier says, "Prisoners kept their minds active by memorizing the names of their fellow prisoners. We were not

65

allowed any writing material, so memorization was the only way we could keep track of each other. By 1970, I had memorized 350 names."

To help them remember, they would use limericks, poems, children stories, rhymes, songs, whatever worked. These names eventually got back to the American authorities, and would prove to be of vital importance.

Since the US government didn't know the fate of many of the missing, they were labeled as Missing in Action (MIA), leaving their families and loved ones in a special hellish kind of limbo. Captain Cordier was listed MIA for his first three years in captivity. Meanwhile, the North Vietnamese never released the names of all the American prisoners they held until the release of prisoners in 1973.

Why, one might ask? For one thing, the NV knew that at the war's end, *they* would be held responsible for the fate of the POWs. Not so for the MIAs, since officially they had never been prisoners in the first place. If an MIA disappeared, nothing could be proved. Once their status changed from MIA to POW, then the NV officially became responsible for their fate.

The Cost of Freedom

Chapter 8

"Initially, some of the POWs were rightfully fearful of additional torture and as a defense technique told the North Vietnamese what they thought they wanted to hear. This was a big mistake because the NV, thinking they had someone willing to cooperate, would push the guy over the line to do something dishonorable or disloyal. Most would pull back and resist, but it was much more difficult at that point and it took more courage to adhere to the Code of Conduct (CoC) than if they had held the line from the beginning."

The Code of Conduct is an ethics guide and a set of rules that American soldiers are expected to follow if captured. It is considered an important part of U.S. military doctrine and tradition, but is not formal military law, such as the Geneva Conventions. It evolved out of the Korean War experience, where commanders saw many soldiers collaborate and submit to brainwashing. It has undergone slight stylistic changes over the years. Here is the current Code of Conduct:

Article I: I am an American, fighting in the forces which guard my country and our way of life. I am prepared to give my life in their defense.

Article II: I will never surrender of my own free will. If in command, I will never surrender the members of my command while they still have the means to resist.

Article III: If I am captured, I will continue to resist by all means available. I will make every effort to escape and aid others to escape. I will accept neither paroles nor special favors from the enemy.

Article IV: If I become a prisoner of war I will keep faith with my fellow prisoners. I will give no information or take part in any action which might be harmful to my comrades. If I am senior, I will take command. If not, I will obey the lawful orders of those appointed over me and will back them up in every way.

Article V: When questioned, should I become a prisoner of war, I am required to give my name, rank, and serial number, and date of birth. I will evade answering further questions to the upmost of my ability. I will make no oral or written statements disloyal to my country and its allies or harmful to their cause.

Article VI: I will never forget that I am an American, fighting for freedom, responsible for my actions, and dedicated to the principles which made my country free. I will trust in my God and in the United States of America.

The North Vietnamese were nothing, if not forcefully persistent. Once they sensed, rightly or wrongly, that they had someone they could use, they wouldn't let go, and they had lots of ways to apply pressure. Both carrot and stick.

The stick consisted of what you've already been reading about within these pages. The POWs were often instructed that if their attitudes did not improve (i.e. if they didn't cooperate), they would continue to be 'severely punished.' It is interesting to note that whenever the POWs were threatened with punishment, it was nearly always <u>severe</u> punishment. These two words were routinely used as one. On this count, the POWs learned that the enemy would keep his word. Through extensive and extended torture, all American POWs eventually 'cooperated', albeit in ways that were for the most part completely meaningless and of no real help to the enemy at all.

A few of them, however, would need no such drastic convincing. A carrot would be sufficient. The main carrot offered was most attractive: freedom itself. Those deserving such favor would have a good chance of going home 'early'. First, they would have to admit to, and apologize for, all the crimes they had committed against the Vietnamese people. They also would need to tell the world of America's true imperialistic goals of the war.

At that time, Vice Admiral James B. Stockdale was the POW senior ranking officer (the SRO). He brought up an important point: "It's not generally known, but Americans held in Hanoi were free to go anytime, provided that prisoner recorded disloyal anti-American tapes and that he was willing to violate our prisoner's underground organization's self-imposed creed of comradeship: Accept no parole or amnesty; we all go home together."[1]

Through the tap-code communication system, Stockdale instructed the men how to respond to these 'go-home-early' offers. It was simple: no one was to accept early release. This was one of their foundational policies, which would come to be known as 'plums'. Plums were the guidance policies put out by the senior officers. To the vast majority of POWs, the idea of early release was as intolerable as it was to Stockdale. They were determined that if a deal was struck for one to leave, it would have to be for ALL to leave, and in the order of their respective capture dates.

Every man would have to make his own decision. For a very few, the carrot would win out. Altogether, there would be eleven who would sign up with North Vietnam's agenda. They would help Hanoi with their propaganda campaign, and brutal interrogation or torture methods wouldn't even be necessary.

Some POWs produced especially nasty and venomous anti-war and anti-American material. Especially disgusting to the other POWs was what they called The Bob & Ed Show. This was a talky anti-American taped broadcast over the prison PA system. Navy Commander Robert Schweitzer and Marine Lieutenant Colonel Edison Miller were the two collaborators who began this travesty. These two were especially contemptuous of the Code of Conduct, and scornful of the war and America in general. They 'performed' in-house for their fellow POWs, who in turn detested them with a vengeance. Rewarded for their 'good attitudes' (read unashamed cooperation), the NV provided them with special treatment, including good food, comfortable living conditions, beer, ice cream, Vietnamese dinners, front-row seats at a local circus, no 'severe punishment', and eventually early release. They were wisely kept isolated from the other POWs.

Col. Cordier remembers this period well. He says, "The culmination of the V's screening program yielded eleven collaborators who accepted a propaganda release and went home early, before those shot down before them. This was in direct violation of the Code of Conduct and a thumb of the nose to the rest of us left behind. One of these wretched men, a Korean War Ace, told others in the camp 'it's every man for himself—I'm going home any way I can.' Needless to say, these men are held in contempt and are held incommunicado by the rest of the POWs to this day."

In North Vietnam at this time, there were altogether 409 American officers (the majority pilots), 157 enlisted men and 28 men who died in captivity in North Vietnam. Among all these, only those eleven would align themselves with the NV, and so become outcasts to the others.

The first propaganda release of three 'turncoats' would be on August 2, 1968. Another three were released in August 1969, and the last three went out in September 1972. Before their return to America, having sold their honor for a mere four or five months of freedom, this latter group would 'make the rounds' in North Vietnam.

Newsweek Magazine reported, "Greeted in the North Vietnamese capital with bouquets of gladiolus and roses-and an air raid alert-the visitors met the three freed POWs in an emotionally televised ceremony the next day ... for two days they were paraded around on well-publicized tours of the war-devastated countryside ... (they) expressed their thanks to the North Vietnamese during a farewell banquet for their treatment while in prison ... Laden with gifts and souvenirs, including cigarette boxes made with the metal of downed U.S. planes, these Hanoi three finally left on their circuitous journey home..."[2]

One of the men in the second group to get early release was honorable. Seaman Doug Hedgal accidentally fell overboard from the destroyer he was serving on during the night and was able to stay afloat until morning when he was picked up by a NV fishing boat. They turned him over to the authorities and he soon found himself in prison in Hanoi. Once the NV realized he wasn't one of the "Yankee Air Pirates", they informed him that he might get to go home before the others. Doug realized that there was a 'go-home' program for those who collaborated, and made it known that he didn't want to be associated with them. The SRO told him that here was our one chance to get out many of our names, so it was his duty to memorize as many names as he could to get this information back to the states. Doug applied himself and memorized over 250 names which he relayed to our military services as soon as he returned. Ken Cordier's name was among them. Ken had been listed MIA until that time, so for three years his family didn't know if he was dead or alive.

~~~~~~~~~~~~

One last thing of interest here. During Christmas time of 1966, Hanoi Hannah was playing some POW Christmas messages to their families on her radio show. Looking back now, Col. Cordier states, "After hearing these for several days (they were being played on the PA system otherwise known as Camp Radio) I mentioned to 'The Elf' that I had heard these tapes and wondered

71

if I might be allowed to make such a greeting to my family. He indicated that it would be possible, but first I must demonstrate good attitude and by positive acts help to work for ending the war. Specifically, I could write a letter to my Congressman and Senators demanding the U.S. to immediately withdraw from Vietnam and let the Vietnamese people settle their own affairs. I thanked him and said maybe next year.

At that time, I by no means thought the war would last another year. Later on I learned that the men allowed to make those Christmas tapes were all among those whose names had been previously released. For the rest of us, it was just a tool to pressure us to give them propaganda and a measure of our resolve to resist."

Web of Deceit

Chapter 9

*"Oh! What a tangled web we weave,
when first we practice to deceive."*
From the play "Marmion", by Sir Walter Scott

Two years into Ken's imprisonment and one year before Ho Chi Minh's death, things turned from bad to worse. "But", one might ask, "how could things get any worse? Had North Vietnam come up with some new, superior military strategy?" No, there was never any fundamental change in their approach. Facing the most powerful nation in the world, their strategy was always quite simple: make the war long, bloody, and expensive: a war of attrition. Through this they hoped to turn American public opinion against the war, thereby forcing Uncle Sam to pull out. After all, they knew they could always count on the American press to support their agenda. There was no need to change strategy.

Perhaps there was a sudden increase of decisive enemy victories? No, in fact United States soldiers won every significant battle they fought during the entire Vietnam War. No, it was something even worse.

Four days before the Presidential election (October 31, 1968), President Johnson announced over nationwide radio and television an especially damaging direction for the war. "I have now ordered that all air, naval, and artillery bombardment of North Vietnam cease as of 8am, Washington time, Friday morning. I have reached this decision on the basis of the developments in the Paris talks. And I have reached this decision in the belief that this action can lead to progress toward a peaceful settlement of the Vietnam War." In reality, this was a grandstand play to show the American people that the Democrat party would be the one to bring peace to Vietnam. Some of the POWs thought that this was a good development which might lead to a relaxation of the bad treatment. Unfortunately, stopping the bombing would prove to be disastrous not only to America's war effort, but especially to those in captivity: the POWs.

Apparently, the Communists took this announcement as a sign of weakness and lack of resolve. The POWs always got bad news over the Camp Radio, and when Ken heard it, he exploded to his cellmates, "The blank-blank has sold us down the river. He didn't even ask for a list of our names, much less a guarantee of our treatment according to the Geneva Conventions."

Ken refers to LBJ unaffectionately as 'Lying Baines Johnson'. There are substantial and direct reasons for such a moniker, including LBJ's lies regarding both the beginning of the 1964 bombing, and stopping it in 1968. The press was, as usual, a willing accomplice to both. Between the press and the government, it was hard to keep all the lies straight.

On August 5, 1964, the Washington Post headline stated, "American Planes Hit North Vietnam After Attack on Our Destroyers; Move Taken to Halt New Aggression." That same day, the New York Times front page 'reported', "President Johnson has ordered retaliatory action against gunboats and 'certain supporting facilities in North Vietnam' after renewed attacks against American destroyers in the Gulf of Tonkin."

In reality, there was no "new aggression" by North Vietnam. There were no "renewed attacks against American destroyers." However by reporting official claims as absolute truth, the press had just opened the floodgates to the Vietnam War. As the days passed, a pattern would emerge and gain strength: continuous government lies would quickly be passed down to a gullible public, like, as Gen. Patton would say, "like crap through a goose", by an arrogant and agenda-driven press.

The day he heard about Johnson's 1968 speech, he instantly deduced the implications, providing for "...my lowest morale since the day I was shot down. Through secret meetings our government knew in early 1967 that we were being tortured and abused. The simplest response of the Geneva conventions is that they are obliged to give a list of the names of the people being held. In my case, I was listed as Missing-In-Action for another year after the bombing halt.

"The Vietnamese seemed to think that since our government made no mention of us in return for halting the bombing, they could do anything they wanted with us. So they took off on a new path of punishing us. We were the worst kind of criminals, and needed to be punished."

The form of punishments began to change. A previous popular form of "minor beatings" was what the POWs called "facials". Capt. Cordier clarifies, "These weren't Mary Kay facials. They made us kneel down, and put our head at their waist level. They'd take off a rubber tire sandal and whack you across the head and face for minor infractions. They didn't have to get permission to do that. These 'facials' would give way to floggings. Floggings meant that you had to strip naked and lay face down on the ground. They would get a guard on either side of you with a truck fan belt, and lay it to you."

Flogging with Fan Belt

"We learned about the stripes that Jesus experienced, because when we went back to our cell, our back would be covered with red Xs, all the way from the shoulders to the butt. That wore us down. They would flog you for anything. One of my cellmates got flogged for looking disrespectfully at a guard. The guard didn't like him and he just wanted an excuse to give him a whipping.

"I took 15 lashes for sleeping in the nude. A guard came around during one oppressively hot night, popped open the inspection hatch, and shined his flashlight on me. I was sleeping nude, trying to get a little relief from the heat. I was hauled off to the quiz shack where I was accused of showing disrespect for the Camp Commander, for which I was duly punished.

"This is how we lived during that spring and summer of 1969. It was really hard to stay optimistic. We still rarely got outside. We had very minimal rations, and the floggings were all just grinding us down. As we used to say, it was making old men out of young men."

Bow Down to Me

Chapter 10

*"A nation's culture resides in the hearts and
in the soul of its people."*
Mahatma Gandhi

*"'And it shall be from new moon to new moon
And from Sabbath to Sabbath. All mankind will
come to bow down before Me,' says the LORD."*
Isaiah 66:23

Traditions stretching back hundreds, if not thousands of years, remain deeply ingrained in Vietnamese culture. Bowing is a good example. Westernization is slowly changing this, but for most Vietnamese, bowing still remains an integral part of socialization. It is not only a greeting, but an essential sign of respect. For someone to intentionally disregard this basic courtesy shows disrespect not only to the person, but also to their family, up to and including their deceased ancestors.

This would become a problem for the American POWs. Colonel Cordier remembers: "We were told that we must bow to any Vietnamese who came to our cell, or whom we might encounter outdoors (on the rare occasion we were out of our cell). We took bowing as a demeaning act. I just hated it, and so did a lot of the other guys. We could have saved ourselves some grief if we had just gone along with it, but for whatever reason, we always resisted it, and did so in ways that didn't do us any good or accomplish anything. They certainly were not going to let us get away with being disrespectful by refusing to bow or giving a sloppy bow.

"We had a turn-key we called McGoo who had a lazy eye which was always looking at an odd angle. So I would focus on his bad eye when bowing. One day, when I was being locked in my cell, I had my bowl of rice in my hand and stared at his lazy eye as I bowed, allowing my other arm to dangle limply. He had had enough of my insolence, and in a flash, kicked the rice bowl out of my hand, scattering the contents all over the floor. There was no way to recover hundreds of grains of rice and separate them from the dirt and dust. In this case, I had to go without my staple for one meal—not worth the loss, even it if was a small emotional victory.

"In North Vietnam, dog meat is considered a delicacy; it is a special treat enjoyed on the Tet holiday, much like turkey in America on Thanksgiving. Every year, several dogs would show up in camp a couple of months before Tet, and the camp kitchen would feed them and fatten them up. The guards treated them badly, kicking and sadistically abusing them. We heard the dogs scream and howl and called it 'tenderizing the dogs'.

"One chilly February day I was being marched off to 'quiz' (interrogation) at bayonet point, when one of the pups trotted across my path. It was a part of the camp regulations that you had to bow politely to every Vietnamese. I stopped, came to attention, and performed a stiff, deep bow to the dog. The guard knew immediately what I was inferring. He started yelling at me and gave me a hard chop to the ribs with his rifle butt. I'm lucky I didn't get a cracked rib. As soon as we got to the interrogation room he told the interrogator ('The Elf' for this session) about my insolent behavior.

"The Elf started screaming and yelling at me, 'You'll never go home! You are the worst criminal!' He went through the usual diatribe of my crimes against the Vietnamese people, my bad attitude, the punishment I deserved and would receive. Blah, blah, blah—but he did not hit me. He then called the guard and told me to return to my cell and think about my crimes.

"This turned out very well for me. In my mind I got in a resistance lick against bowing, and avoided shivering on a stool for an hour while the interrogator gave me a propaganda lecture. Plus, I had the entertainment bonus of tapping a description of the incident to my neighboring cellmates. Tales of resisting the enemy sometimes resulted in boosting the morale of fellow prisoners. Other than a couple of sore ribs, I got off with no physical abuse. Anyway, as I used to say in those days, 'If you don't get a beating once in a while, you're not getting away with enough.'"

Ironically, supreme communist dictator Ho Chi Minh would himself be the catalyst for change in prison-bowing etiquette. But not in a way he could have foreseen. On September 2, 1969, Uncle Ho went to his eternal home, wherever that may be. This would foretell the beginning of many positive changes for all the POWs. Ken continues: "After a month of mandatory national mourning, you could tell there was a new administration running the show. Right away they came around and knocked all the bricks out of the windows. Then they took everybody out of irons. There had always been guys in irons for various punishments. They started letting us outside for 2 hours a day, and not limiting our bathing.

"As a result of these changes, we got very optimistic. We thought they must be getting close to repatriating us. Not only did they take everyone out of irons, they told us that we should exercise to keep our health. What a change! And finally, they told us we didn't have to bow anymore."

Even with these positive changes, actual freedom was still a long way off. Captain Cordier was roughly only half-way through his prison ordeal.

Sơn Tây Raid

Chapter 11

"The Lord sets prisoners free."
Psalm 146:7

Nine months following the 1969 autumn death of Ho Chi Minh, "they moved us to a new camp where the physical conditions were better. We called this 'Camp Faith'. Here the windows were barred but open, so there was ventilation. We were allowed more outside time. We made a little jogging track, so we could jog barefoot, having picked out all the pebbles and stones to make it smoother."

With the improvement in treatment, "everybody got optimistic. They thought, 'Well they must be sending us home soon.' A lot of the POWs were just ecstatic. They said, 'This is so wonderful.'"

"We learned from the Vietnamese prisoners on the other side of camp that there had been a grab attempt to liberate the camp at Sơn Tây. Some of the men thought, 'Oh, that's great! The government hasn't forgotten us!' But I looked at it as a source of pessimism. I thought, 'How foolish. If the US government would mount a high-risk operation that close to Hanoi, then there must be no foreseeable negotiated release for us, and we were going to be here for a very long time.'"

Ken remembers well the early pre-dawn hours of Nov. 20-21, 1970: "It was nighttime, and it was dark. We had been at Camp Faith for about three months. All of a sudden, there was a lot of noise! We heard jets in after-burner, anti-aircraft fire, SAMs shooting off and Triple A (anti-aircraft artillery)! Then it got quiet. We were really thrilled, and thought, 'The bombing is back on!'"

But it wasn't. In fact, there hadn't been any bombing north of the 19th parallel since LBJ ordered his Halloween halt in late '68. After that, the Paris Peace talks dragged on and on. North Vietnam wouldn't be the target of intense bombing for another two and a half years.

This nighttime bombing was strange, since before the 1968 bombing halt, they had almost always taken place during the daytime. Nonetheless, for all the commotion it created, it's easy to understand how the POWs thought the bombing must be back on. In reality, it was the Sơn Tây raid. This was a mission whereby Special Forces soldiers were to locate, protect and rescue all prisoners located at the Sơn Tây POW camp; and to kill any guards that might interfere. Commanding officer Colonel Arthur D. "Bull" Simons succinctly put it this way to his team of Green Berets, *"We are going to rescue 70 American POWs, maybe more, from a camp called Sơn Tây. This is something American prisoners have a right to expect from their fellow soldiers. The target is 23 miles west of Hanoi."* [1] It was in the most heavily defended area of the country, close to MIG interceptor air bases, and carefully positioned anti-aircraft artillery and surface-to-air missile sites. There were over 12,000 North Vietnamese soldiers stationed within five miles of the prison.

"The Raid, Blue Boy Element" by Michael Nikiporenko[2]

This top-secret mission was carried out by 56 U.S. Army Special Forces soldiers and 98 airmen aboard 28 aircraft. Months of intelligence gathering, mission planning and meticulous training preceded the mission. A full-size replica of the prison was constructed and live-fire training was conducted. Personnel were selected from more than 500 volunteers. Training took place around the clock, with joint training at night. Different portions of the rescue had been practiced 170 times, including every imaginable contingency plan. Except one. What if no POWs were found in the camp? Murphy's Law[3] being firmly in place, this was indeed what the Green Berets found. A short time before the raid, the POWs in the Sơn Tây camp had all been moved to the new camp named 'Camp Faith'.

The total time from the beginning to the end of the assault was just 26 minutes. As the Raiders withdrew from the area, North Vietnam fired more than 36 surface-to-air missiles at the aircraft. None were hit. Between 100–200 North Vietnamese soldiers were killed, while only two Americans were slightly wounded. But no POWs were found.

"They thought we were heroes, but most of us that were the Raiders, pulled our one-year tour in Vietnam and then came home. These POWs were there 5-to-7 years. They carried on the battle. They did not give up. When you compare that to what was going on at home—protests, people going to Canada to avoid military service—while the POWs were rotting and suffering and being tortured against the laws of warfare. They were the heroes, not us."[4]

To the casual observer, the raid had been a failure. However, as things began to be evaluated, it turned out that the results were actually very positive. First of all, the attempt to rescue prisoners brought the world's attention to the inhumane treatment of the American POWs. Secondly, and perhaps inadvertently, it sent a message to the Russians and the Chinese assisting the North Vietnamese that America had not forgotten their prisoners. Thirdly, it showed the NV that they were not safe anywhere from

American reprisals. Lastly, and most importantly for the POWs, the raid altered how the North Vietnamese housed, treated, and interacted with them.

The change in treatment began almost immediately. "Two days after the raid, shaken by this unexpected and brazen attack, the NV loaded us into trucks and took us back to Hanoi. It scared them so badly that the US, the all-powerful US, might come in, grab us all up and take us home. So they emptied all the South Vietnamese prisoners currently occupying the old French prison we called the 'Hanoi Hilton', and put us all in this one compound that held 350 men in seven large rooms. We didn't even know that this part of the prison existed, because no Americans had ever been held there before. Instead, we had been held in the area we called Heartbreak Hotel, and New Guy Village, where all the new prisoners were brought to be interrogated.

"There were men who were in isolation for years, unable to see or speak to other Americans. The only way they could communicate was to tap on the walls. All of a sudden these people in isolation ended up in the 'Hanoi Hilton' in a room together with as many as 50 other captives, their comrades-in-arms. There, the ones in poor health, could be cared for by the others.

"We really had a surge of optimism as a result of this move. We were so excited that we stayed up all night talking. The guards would come around, bang on the bars and yell, 'Keep silent! Sleep!' We just ignored them.

"The guards realized the magnitude of this move and decided not to take any reprisals. The POW treatment and food improved as well. A side benefit of our reorganization in the prison was that for a few weeks there was limited communication between some South Vietnamese prisoners and the US POWs. This was where we first heard about the Sơn Tây raid."

Was this the light at the end of the tunnel? With the Sơn Tây raid, Uncle Ho's death, improved living conditions, and being put all together for the first time since being captured, things appeared to be on a positive vector. But the tunnel would prove to be unusually long. As Ken says, "Little did we know that another 2 ½ years would pass before our release would be negotiated."

Live and Let Live

Chapter 12

"If you're going through hell, keep going."
Attributed to Winston Churchill

The move to the 'Hanoi Hilton' marked the beginning of a new and distinct period in the saga of the American POWs in Vietnam. Ken says, "We were never given any books, except for occasional propaganda pieces. I never saw a Bible, much less had my own personal copy, like the terrorists at Guantanamo have their own Quran. We never had pencil and paper to write with, nor dictionaries or language books. All we had was what was in our brains." Nevertheless, a series of ad hoc courses and self-entertainment emerged among the inmates based on their previous knowledge and experience.

"We used Yankee ingenuity to create writing paper out of toilet paper and chalk out of little chips of orange roofing tile. You don't have to have a chalk board on the wall; the floor worn smooth by 60 to 70 years of prisoners pacing back and forth made an excellent chalkboard. So for math, chemistry and technical subjects, men would cluster around the teacher, who would write on the floor. If a guard came along we would rub it off with our rubber tire sandals and act like nothing had happened. This kept our minds busy. We had all sorts of subjects. If you had a course that you could teach, or an area of expertise, you were obliged to organize it and share it.

"Languages like German, French and Spanish were popular. We had courses in math, history, science and geography. It was amazing the breadth of knowledge that we had in that group.

85

"Several men designed houses in their minds and were able to actually have these constructed when they were free men. Some of the accomplished golfers in the group gave golf lessons, using a bamboo stick and an imagined ball. After their release from prison, some took up golf for the first time, using what they learned in Hanoi.

"We even had a Toastmasters club. Those who had been in Toastmasters reconstructed the program and we went through it. Yankee ingenuity played here, also. We stacked a couple of water cans to make a podium. The 'ah counter' marked ah's with an orange clay tile, and the time keeper closed his eyes and counted 'a thousand one, a thousand two...' until the allotted time for a speech, table topic, or an evaluation was up. To be properly and professionally dressed, we would press our stripped prison pajamas beforehand by carefully folding them and stacking blankets on top.

"Entertainment presented another challenge. One of our cellmates, Jerry Venanzi, had worked as a movie usher through college and had seen all the new movies over and over. We called him 'The Projector' and we passed many evenings listening to his fairly accurate recap of a movie. Others told movies and books and if they couldn't remember as well as Jerry, they would collaborate with others who had seen the movie or read the book. Books were turned into movies with roles for favorite actors and actresses assigned. Taking 'Hanoi license', most of the books and movies were X-rated by the time they were told.

"A few of the men received packs of playing cards in their packages from home. The NV got suspicious that messages were laminated in these cards, so they took them all away and replaced them with Vietnamese cards which were of a cheap pasteboard material. After normal shuffling, the spots would wear off making them virtually useless. So we developed an alternate way of shuffling the deck by dealing out nine cards, repeating on top of these, becoming nine stacks, and then randomly restacking the deck.

"Favorite card games included poker and bridge. Every Sunday afternoon, we would have a duplicate bridge tournament. Some of the made up conventions were very interesting and creative. One needs to be careful when playing bridge with an ex-POW.

"Another popular game was backgammon. We had to make the game using laminated pieces of toilet paper smeared with rice paste for the board. The dice and pieces were made with stale bread which had turned sour on the inside. We picked out the gummy insides and worked them until they had the consistency of modeling clay. After forming the pieces, the challenge was to allow them to dry and harden without the rats getting to them. Once they were hard, the rats wouldn't bother them. Cigarette ashes mixed in the dough produced black dice. With a nail to scratch an indentation, filling those with a dab of toothpaste, spots would be made.

"It was around this time that we heard on the VoV (Voice of Vietnam) that Cuba had donated a shipload of sugar to Vietnam. We started seeing a scoop of sugar show up on our tin plates and I thought, 'Hmm, sugar water ferments.' So I got some guys to form a wine club with me. We had these one liter teapots that we had kept our water ration in, but when they moved us into the bigger compounds, they started giving us these large 20-liter aluminum cans for our water, but didn't take our teapots away.

"We had these teapots, and also we'd just gotten some packages from home. They allowed the families to mail international post packages for us. Actually, it was just a black market scam, because at that time there were 1,800 MIA families sending packages, but only around 400 POWs receiving packages. The camp authorities kept the remaining packages for their own use, or sale of all the American goodies on the local black market.

"A couple of my cellmates got dried fruit and raisins. This was a good thing to put in the package, because the Vietnamese didn't steal that. (By stealing, I mean for example, one of my 4.4 pound boxes had only a little tin of hard candy and a pair of jockey shorts. I asked the officer who gave the box, 'What happened to the rest of it?' The next time I got a package there was no box, just the few items I received.

"I made sugar water in the teapot, and bit the dried fruit and raisins into small pieces. I knew that the yeast in my saliva would start the fermentation process. I set them up on a window ledge to age, and sure enough they started fermenting. In a few days there was foam on the top. After about ten days, I deemed it ready and scooped the foam off the teapots. We had 'Happy Hour' that Friday night. It wasn't very good, but it had some alcohol in it.

"All this made the time pass. As long as we didn't make noise or create a disturbance, the guards mostly left us alone. We called it the 'live and let live' period." Things seemed to drag on endlessly. Never being able to count on anything made life extremely difficult.

"Part of the uncertainty was simply not knowing how long you were going to be there. By this time, I'd been there nearly four years. So I thought, 'I'm going to pick a date to count down on when I think I'll be released.' I made it far enough in the future, that surely we would be out by then. I picked July 4, 1976, the Bi-Centennial as the day I'd be free. Well, my optimism paid off because I got out on March 4, 1973, so I got out early!"

The Beginning of the End

Chapter 13

"I'll make him an offer he can't refuse."
Don Vito Corleone, from the 1972 movie <u>The Godfather</u>

"Months were ticking off for nearly a year and a half with no change to our situation. Then on a Sunday morning (April 16, 1972) we heard jets in after-burner, bombs exploding, anti-aircraft and air raid sirens. We were jumping up and down and cheering and singing 'God Bless America'! What a day! We knew if they were bombing Hanoi, the war was back on for real."

Finally, after a 3 ½ year lull, America bombed both Haiphong and Hanoi. Eighteen B-52s and about one hundred U.S. Navy and Air Force fighter-bombers struck supply dumps near Haiphong's harbor, while sixty fighter-bombers hit petroleum storage facilities near Hanoi. But that was just the beginning. President Nixon would continue to intensify the bombing until the Vietnamese at the Paris Peace Conference began negotiating in earnest. As if to make a point, that same afternoon another wave of American planes bombed Hanoi again. White House spokesmen announced that the United States would now bomb military targets anywhere in Vietnam—whatever it took to help the South Vietnamese defend themselves against the communist onslaught. Both South Vietnam and the POWs celebrated, and rightfully so.

Actually, these actions were part of the U.S. response to the North Vietnamese offensive which had begun on March 30th. They had launched a massive invasion, called the Nguyen Hue Offensive (more commonly known to Americans as the "Easter Offensive."), that was designed to strike the knockout blow that would win the war for the communists. The North Vietnamese effort included more than 120,000 troops and approximately 1,200 tanks and other armored vehicles. The South Vietnamese fought for their very survival, and this time, they prevailed against the invaders with the help of U.S. advisors and massive American airpower.[1]

Ken continues, "So now everybody got optimistic again because President Nixon was carrying the war to these people in their capital city. Now maybe something would happen!

"Some of the bombs were getting pretty close. Plaster would fall off the prison ceiling, and the ground would shake. Dust would jump an inch off the floor. It was really hard to describe. If you've never been in a bombing raid, I wouldn't advise it, but it *was* very exciting.

"This daily bombing of Hanoi continued for a month. Then on the 15th of May, the NV loaded half of us on trucks and took off for parts unknown. We drove all day and part of the night, and finally arrived in a mountainous jungle area, at what we found out later was a camp five kilometers from the Chinese border. We called it 'Dog Patch'. It was very remote and primitive with no electricity. Whereas cells in the other Vietnamese prisons were lit 24 hours a day, at 'Dog Patch' they were perpetually dark at night.

"There were some advantages. For one thing, we would not be around for Jane Fonda's appearance, although we would hear about it soon enough. She showed up in July, displaying her support for the North Vietnamese, thus earning both her new nickname "Hanoi Jane" and the undying enmity of Americans everywhere; not the least being the POWs themselves.

"Hanoi Jane" aided and abetted the enemy, as documented by her own words, and many photos of her sitting on North Vietnamese anti-aircraft guns, taken in Hanoi in July, 1972. A few hundred yards from the photo site below, American POWs had been subjected to all manner of torture at the 'Hanoi Hilton'. Fonda called returning POWs "hypocrites and liars," adding,

"These were not men who had been tortured. These were not men who had been starved. These were not men who had been brainwashed ... Pilots were saying it was the policy of the Vietnamese and that it was systematic. I believe that's a lie."

"Hanoi Jane" consorting with the enemy.

Of course, at this point, Hanoi Jane would just be a side show for the POWs. They sensed that the war must be drawing to a close. The NV knew that it was in their best interests to keep their prisoners alive and well, so conditions continued to improve.

Meanwhile, the extremely primitive living found at 'Dog Patch' provided another unexpected advantage. Imagine living in close confinement with people you didn't choose, and perhaps didn't even like. Imagine being forced to live together in such intimate and desperate circumstances, sometimes for years. Under such circumstances, living alone might be seen as a luxury only dreamed about. Now, short term solitary confinement would become something desired, not feared.

"We lived in this building that had seven two-man cells, and at the end there was one solitary cell. We got the guards to agree that we could take turns being in solitary. We'd take turns, one week at a time. It was really nice being quiet and by yourself, and not having to listen to anyone else chattering or using the bucket during the night.

Some remains of 'Dog Patch'. Photo by Alan Fox, 2007

"Because there was no electricity, we had to get up and go to bed with the chickens. It wasn't all that bad, because they told us that when the war was over, we'd go back to Hanoi, and in the meantime they would try to make our conditions better. They allowed us outside in our little courtyards all day, but we still couldn't communicate with the other cell blocks. The food improved. The soup had mixed vegetables and the broth was thickened and good. I'd probably enjoy it today. The best change in the diet was getting a tuna-sized can of Russian mackerel packed in oil, shared among 3 men daily. We carefully divided it and found it to be very tasty on rice."

A few more months passed with no electricity, therefore no radio, no news, and no propaganda. Another Christmas season approached. But that Christmas, the Christmas of 1972, would be different. That year Santa Claus had made special plans for the POWs.

"The guards told us that if we would behave, and not make a disturbance, they would allow us out in the area in between the buildings and we could visit and celebrate Christmas with our fellow prisoners. That was the first time such a thing had ever happened. We got to see all the POWs from the other buildings."

What a wonderful Christmas present. But it was just the stocking hanging from the chimney. The best gifts were yet to come. While many of the POWs were reveling in the unexpected pleasure of celebrating Christmas together for the first time since their captivity, an interrogator came around with the Hanoi newspaper and on the centerfold was a big picture of a B-52 dropping a string of bombs. He said, "See, fresh American war crimes. You'll never go home."

A most welcome sight…

"Operation Linebacker II" was conducted during December 18 - 29, 1972. It was also labeled with several informal names such as "The December Raids" and "The Christmas Bombings". Unlike "Operation Rolling Thunder" and "Operation Linebacker" interdictions, "Linebacker II" was to be a 'maximum effort' bombing campaign to destroy major target complexes in the Hanoi and Haiphong areas. It would be the largest heavy bomber strikes launched by the US Air Force since the end of World War II.

It had been a momentous year. 1972 was drawing to a close with a 'bang'. *Time* Magazine's 'Men of the Year' were none other than Richard Nixon and Henry Kissinger. The number one rated TV show was *All in the Family*. The 1972 Oscar for best movie went to *The Godfather*. Somehow, this seems appropriate, as President Nixon had just made an offer that the NV couldn't refuse: The '72 Christmas Bombing campaign.

"It was like seeing Santa Claus coming down the chimney because we knew if the B-52s were bombing Hanoi, it would probably be over very soon." Indeed it was. Merry Christmas.

'Operation Homecoming'

Chapter 14

"I am with you, and will rescue you, declares the Lord."
Jeremiah 1:8

"Imagine you're imprisoned in a cage; imagine the cage surrounded by the smell of feces; imagine the rotted food you eat is so infested with insects that to eat only a few is a blessing; imagine knowing your life could be taken by one of your captors on a whim at any moment; imagine you are subjected to mental and physical torture designed to cause intense pain not only of your body but of your spirit. That was the lot of a prisoner in North Vietnam. Then imagine one day, after seemingly endless disappointment, you are given a change of clothes and lined up to watch an American plane land to return you home. That was 'Operation Homecoming'."[1]

Three weeks later, on January 20, 1973, "They loaded us all on trucks, and back to Hanoi we went, back to the Hanoi Hilton, back to the old compound. They assigned us to rooms according to our shoot-down date. After we were there for a few days, they had us all form up in the courtyard, the only time this ever happened. They said, 'Arrange yourselves in a military fashion.' So we did. Each cellblock of 50 to 60 men (we called them squadrons) all lined up in rank and file. I'd say we looked like a pretty motley crew in our stripped pajamas and rubber tire sandals."

Unidentified POWs arranged in 'a military fashion'.

"Then the camp commander came out and read something in Vietnamese, and an interpreter translated it to English. It was the protocol for the release of prisoners. We knew at that point when we were finally going home. The first group went out on February 14th; I was in the second group which was released on March 4th.

"It was agonizing waiting for that date, but we made the best of it. We had a lot of things to talk about: what we were going to do when we got home, speculations about our families, and so forth. Most of us hardly knew anything about the situation back home with our wives and kids.

"Finally, March 4th arrived. We got up, folded our blankets and mosquito nets for the last time, and some even bathed with cold water from the tank in our bathing area. I always hated the cold baths, and commented that I would wait a few hours for a hot shower at Clark Air Base. The V ushered us into a room where we were issued our 'go home clothes' which consisted of cotton slacks, shirt and a light jacket. We were given boxer shorts and a T-shirt for underwear, socks and flimsy shoes which would serve only to make the trip to the airport and look good in the expected photos. Back in our cells, we changed into our new 'uniform'. We were also issued a small gym bag for the personal items we were given: a pack of cigarettes, a small bar of soap, a small towel, a toothbrush and toothpaste.

"At the last minute they told us we could 'take home some souvenirs'. I grabbed my tin cup, striped pajamas, rubber tire sandals and the jockey shorts I was wearing when I was shot down. Those shorts have quite a story themselves. They were the only clothing I had on the trip to Hanoi after being captured and during the initial interrogations. When we were released, I kept them on under my prison clothes and determined I would wear them home.

"During inspections, the V would take away any items not issued by the camp authorities. One time they surprised us and I didn't have time to put them on. The V put all our 'contraband' in a pile in the courtyard. My two roommates distracted the guard while I quickly grabbed my shorts and stuffed them in my pants.

"Over the years the shorts faded and looked pretty nasty. But, they were a symbol of my faith in going home to freedom, and I wore them out of the prison on March 4, 1973. (During an interview back home, I mentioned the shorts. The next day, the local Jockey sales rep took me to breakfast and gave me seven sets of underwear of my choice.)

"We assembled in the New Guy Village courtyard, then marched out the front gate (see below) where we were loaded in buses, and driven to Hanoi's Gia Lam Airport.

Front gate of Hoa Lo Prison ('Hanoi Hilton')

"There, we were lined up according to our shoot-down date. One by one, as each man's name was called, he stepped forward and saluted the receiving officer, an American Brigadier General. He shook our hands and personally welcomed each one of us. We then did a right face and marched out to the C-141 waiting on the ramp, with a big American flag on the tail."

The 'Hanoi Taxis': C-141s

"With no show of emotion, we parted from our N. Vietnamese captors and boarded the aircraft. Talk about proud! Here we were, after all these years of mistreatment and isolation, going out with our heads held high, flying to freedom in a US Air Force airplane; not driven across some crummy bridge in an army truck.

"We marched out to the aircraft and were greeted by two AF flight nurses. The one who greeted me gave me a hug and a big kiss. I said, 'You are the best smelling person I've seen in over six years!' We taxied out to the runway. As soon as we heard the gear come up on takeoff, everybody let loose. We were cheering and hugging each other. It was our first taste of freedom. What a moment!"[1]

Celebration broke out aboard the first "Hanoi Taxi" as it lifted skyward.
This experience would be repeated eight more times in each C-141 flight
that followed.
Colonel Cordier's was on March 4, 1973.

All aircraft had an aeromedical team of two flight nurses and three aeromedical evaluation technicians and a couple of flight surgeons. In addition to the medical and flight crews was an escort for each POW and an *AF News* media team.

On the plane, many of the POWs joked and smoked American cigarettes as they caught up on things they'd missed while in captivity. Most of the escorts would remain with the former POWs all the way to the U.S. Their role would be to serve as an aide, military debriefer and as a source of information for men returning to what in many cases was a vastly different world, with new fashion trends, the women's liberation movement, and much more.

In all, 591 American POWs returned from captivity in 'Operation Homecoming' between February 12 and April 1, 1973.

"He lifted me out of the slimy pit; out of the mud and mire, He set my feet on a rock and gave me a firm place to stand." Psalm 40:2

"Thank God Almighty.
We're Free at Last!"[1]

Chapter 15

"I'm coming home I've done my time
Now I've got to know what is and isn't mine
If you received my letter telling you I'd soon be free
Then you'll know just what to do
If you still want me, if you still want me."[2]
Song: "Tie a Yellow Ribbon Round the Ole Oak Tree" by Tony Orlando

First stop for the POWs was Clark Air Base on Luzon Island in the Philippines. They arrived to a hero's welcome at Clark, where Navy Adm. Noel Gayler, commander of U.S. Forces Pacific, led the greeting party. Speaking to the crowd that lined the tarmac to welcome them, returning Navy Capt. Jeremiah Denton, a senior ranking officer in the corps, elicited cheers as he thanked all who had worked for their release and proclaimed, "God bless America!"

Air Force Lt. Col. Carlyle "Smitty" Harris, who spent almost eight years in captivity, joined the many other POWs who echoed that sentiment. "With six, seven or eight years to think about the really important things in life, a belief in God and country were strengthened in every POW with whom I had contact. My only message is, 'God bless America!'" he said, dismissing assertions in the media that the POWs had been directed to say it. As usual, our agenda-driven media remained consistent throughout all these events. Their full-court press for shaping public opinion in their own image never changed before, during or after the war.

Lt. Col. Harris continued, "Firsthand exposure to a system which made a mockery of religion and where men are unable to know truth made us all appreciate some of the most basic values in 'God Bless America.'"[3]

After settling in at the Clark AB Hospital, the men were met by the Joint Debriefing and Casualty Reporting Center (JDCRC). Colonel Cordier picks up his experience: "Once at Clark, we went directly to the hospital, then up to the rooms they had reserved for us. The first thing we did was…guess… SHOWER! A hot shower!

"One of the greatest pleasures of my life, after not having felt warm water for 6 years and 3 months, was to stand under a hot shower. I did that for about 20 minutes until my fingers were all pruny.

"After that we went down to the cafeteria for our first meal. My first meal was steak and eggs, cooked to order, with a banana split for dessert. That was one of the most memorable meals of my life!"

Captain Ken Cordier, 3rd from the right,
in line for his first meal as a free man.

"While we were waiting in line as they cooked the steaks to order, a couple of the flight surgeons couldn't wait until the next morning to start questioning us. One of them came up to me and started asking questions."

"'What are you looking forward to the most?' he queried.

"'What do you think? I've been locked up. I've haven't seen a woman in 6 years and 3 months. And, oh yeah, a glass of whiskey, please.'

"'Well, I can't help you with the former, but what were you drinking when you got shot down?'

"'Jack Daniels. Black.'

"'Oh, OK,' He said. Later I saw him talking to some other former POWs. When I returned to my room after the meal, there was a quart of Jack Daniels lying on my pillow! I took the lid off and took a pull on it and passed it around to my buddies. Everybody in the rooms around me had heard what was going on, so they all gathered in my room. We made one pass with that bottle and it was empty.

"That was the end of my first day of freedom. We were there for another three days for initial medical treatment and debriefings. Men who had medical issues were seen the first morning. In my case, I had been developing an abscess tooth for the last couple of weeks, and was praying that I would get out in time to save it. My first stop was the dental clinic, where I got a root canal and temporary crown. I got a permanent crown when I got back to the states, and have that tooth to this day. I also got crowns on five teeth which were broken or cracked from biting down of small stones in the rice from the crude milling process.

"Next, beginning the debriefings, there were questions about conditions at the point of our departure, but the first thing they wanted was for us to write down all the names we had memorized. They knew by this time we all had memory 'banks'. Memorization was something that you welcomed to keep your mind active. I had 350 names on my list, and most of the others had that or more. So we wrote out all our names which they cross-referenced. That way we accounted for everyone that was in the system, including the ones who had died up there."

Jim Maddux was one of the U.S. Air Force intelligence officers charged with debriefing the POWs at Clark Air Base. He says, "We didn't know what kind of shape they would be in, so we planned for the worst and hoped for the best.

"There were reports that came from sources in North Vietnam that there had been brainwashing," he says. "We didn't know if they would be like robots. We didn't know if they would be hostile to the United States. But it became readily apparent they were on very solid ground. There were a few cases of men with psychological issues, but 95 percent were pretty well squared away."[2] Fortunately, Colonel Cordier fell into the 'squared away' category.

Homeward Bound

Chapter 16

"Home-ward bound, I wish I was,
Home-ward bound,
Home where my thought's escaping,
Home where my music's playing,
Home where my love lies wait-ing
Si-lent-ly for me."
Simon & Garfunkel, 1966

Paul Simon's song about a homesick boy, playing gigs while missing his girlfriend is a lovely song. But of course, when he wrote it, he hadn't just spent more than six years in Vietnamese prison camps. Ken had been through more than most can imagine.

The three days at Clark Air Base, jam packed with medical examinations and debriefings, would pass quickly. "Then we were all flown back to the states. They split us up into five different regional medical centers where we met our families. As you might imagine, that was quiet an emotional event, meeting my wife and my two kids, who didn't remember me. They were three- and five years old when I left, and ten- and twelve years old when I returned. My parents were there as well. So that was really a memorable homecoming. That marked the beginning of my 'second life.'"

The stress on Ken's family was unimaginable. The problems now in front of them as a family, reintegrating into home life, were enormous and unexpected. On top of that, a young marriage in 1959, even under the best of circumstances, had only a 50/50 chance of survival in the first place.

"Reintegrating into family life was difficult; it was a challenge. My wife didn't do well. She quit her nursing job as soon as I got shot down, and just stayed at home, gained a lot of weight, and became a recluse. Consequently the kids didn't get the upbringing and discipline that they should have had. So we had some problems there.

"One of the things I decided before my release was to keep my mouth shut, as best I can, and not make any criticism or lay down any rules or expectations of my family for at least three months. I stuck to that. I just observed and took notes. Over the next few months I collected a lot of things to talk about.

"I waited about four months until I got my first duty station and a new house. Once I was back on active duty, I called a family meeting. They didn't take to it very well. I didn't realize it at the time, but my wife had severe depression. As soon as I came back, she was ready to turn everything over to me. We needed to work as a team, but we did not. I made an effort to re-integrate with my family, but came to realize that it wasn't working. I was frustrated by my inability to influence my children's behavior, or their mother's values. I couldn't "fix" her illness. For five years I tried to make it work, but was unsuccessful. So I began the painful process of separation and divorce.

"It was not a good time for me, and I flippantly say I'd rather spend another year in Hanoi than live those five years again. In a lot of cases, the POWs weren't prepared for what we had to contend with. It was a day by day struggle. There was a whole spectrum of readjustments. Now back home, some of the guys whose wives were strong and did a good job with the kids, keeping things together, had a much easier time. But then there were the men who got divorced right away. And, to this day, I don't think some of the guys have readjusted. A few still harbor negative feelings, and lots of bitterness. I now consider my readjustment period to be those five years leading up to my divorce."

Of course, the wives and children had been fighting their own battles during this stress-filled period of their lives. The high price they paid is now well documented, and would present some surprises. *"Many of the wives of the POWs reported to researchers from the Center for POW Studies that their greatest surprise during homecoming was how little their husband's basic personalities had actually changed during the long, stressful years of captivity. When the men returned the wives expected much change and found little. The husbands, on the other hand, expected little change in their wives and families, and found much. It is little wonder that a substantial part of the post-repatriation reintegration adjustment occurred within the family arena."*[1]

This story, with many variations, has played out for returning vets and their families throughout history. Surprisingly, however, 85% of the Vietnam vets successfully readjusted to postwar life.[2]

The POWs were a select group of mostly aviators whose suffering had been interminable. They had their own demons to deal with. Such extended trauma and suffering would of course have terrible consequences for some who survived it. While many POW's suffered lasting physical effects from their ordeal, according to a detailed 2002 study, it was found that most of them were not mentally *"... irreparably crippled, indeed...some of them have been resilient in the aftermath of trauma, and may even have benefited in some ways from their toxic experiences..."* They found that, *"...POWs who were older and more educated at the time of capture were less distressed upon first returning home, which also meant that they were better adjusted three decades later. The scientists see age and education as personal resources that these men carried with them as they faced months and even years of imprisonment and hardship."*[3] The average age of the American soldier in Vietnam was 22 years old. Captain Cordier was 29 when first captured and 36 when released.

"The findings concerning torture were mixed, and interesting. Being tortured did, as expected, have significant deleterious effects on these young men's mental health following the war. But as the scientists predicted, physical maltreatment also led to positive

107

appraisals of military experience later on. This is consistent with other findings on resilience and post-traumatic growth, and suggests that surviving physical torture might have salutary consequences that temper the trauma. These soldiers may use their torture experiences to make meaning out of their adversity."[4]

Nonetheless, America's intrepid press was once again front and center in their agenda-driven attempt to slander, smear and betray the military in general; at times portraying them as "baby killers" while in Vietnam, then as dangerous crazies once repatriated. Vets were regularly spit on or had tomatoes and other objects thrown at them. Many were refused serve at public establishments. Worse, many vets received little or no support from the Veterans Administration-an arm of the very government that sent them to war in the first place. [5]

General Vo Nguyen Giap, a brilliant and highly respected leader of the North Vietnam military, later said this in his memoirs: *"What we still don't understand is why you Americans stopped the bombing of Hanoi. You had us on the ropes. If you had pressed us a little harder, just for another day or two, we were ready to surrender! It was the same at the battle of TET. You defeated us! We knew it, and we thought you knew it. But we were elated to notice your media was helping us. They were causing more disruption in America than we could in the battlefields. We were ready to surrender. You had won!"*[6]

General Giap was confirming what many Americans already knew. The Vietnam War was not lost in Vietnam—it was lost at home. His memoirs expose the enormous power of a biased media to cut out the heart and will of the American public. He adds another relevant quote: *"Do not fear the enemy, for they can take only your life. Fear the media, for they will distort your grasp of reality and destroy your honor."*[7]

The POWs, for their part, who had already experienced much worse treatment at the hands of their captors, saw the media for what they were (and still are to this very day), and for the most part just moved on with their lives. Living in bitterness becomes a lifetime wasted in regret and anger—burdened and burdening others. We were created for better things.

"As I walked out the door toward the gate that would lead to my freedom, I knew if I didn't leave my bitterness and hatred behind I'd still be in prison."
Nelson Mandela[8]

God knows the huge problems resulting from harboring bitterness, and the Bible addresses it in a number of places. Paul the Apostle tells us simply: *"Get rid of all bitterness, rage and anger, brawling and slander, along with every form of malice."* (Ephesians 4:31)

However that may be easier said than done. Six years of Vietnamese cruelty, abuse and deprivation could provide fertile ground for bitterness. Fortunately, Ken's foundations run deep and solid, and he was able to move past the large bitterness hurdle. Perception and attitude are key in life, and served him well before, during and after his ordeal.

A couple of years ago during an interview he remarked, "If you are going to play with the big boys, you better be prepared to get hurt, and if it ends up that you are the one hurt, well, that's just the way it played out."[9]

Today he says, "Do I harbor any ill feelings against the Vietnamese? No, as a matter of fact, living in Dallas I've become acquainted with and made friends with a few Vietnamese, and find them to be good people, intelligent and hard working. Of course the ones that made it over here were already successful in their own country. They have a wonderful work ethic and make education a priority. The Vietnamese that have come here after that war are like our European immigrant ancestors a hundred years ago. I've told them many times, 'We're really proud of you, and what you've done since coming here.'

109

"Jesus taught us to forgive. Nonetheless, I must admit that if I ever met face to face with one of the torture boys, I might not be as forgiving as Louis Zamperini was when he met his Japanese tormentor, but I like to think I would try.

"My first trip back to Vietnam was in 1995. I told my wife that I had only seen that country through a bomb sight, and would like to see it on the ground and see what it was we were fighting for. We flew to Saigon with my good friend Bernhard Diehl, who was my Best Man at our wedding in 1980. He was a German civilian who had been working at a hospital in the Central Highlands when he was captured by the VC and taken to Hanoi where he was held for four years. We had a car and driver and drove to Da Nang taking in many historic sites along the way. I was disappointed we were not allowed to visit Cam Ranh Bay, even though I offered a $20 bribe to the gate guard, which was equivalent to a month's pay. Cam Ranh Bay is where I flew out of when I was shot down in 1966, and it was an inactive airfield at the time of my visit.

When some of my fellow POWs heard about my trip, they expressed interest in going along if I went again. So, we organized a trip in 1998 with thirteen POWs, their wives and family members, including my son Louie. This time we flew to Hanoi and visited some of our old prisons including the Hanoi Hilton, the Zoo and Son Tay. Most of the Hilton had been torn down and a high rise building built on the site. The Communists kept the main entrance, a section of wall, and two buildings as a museum, depicting the mistreatment of Vietnamese by the French and their good treatment of the American POWs (in other words, pure propaganda). From Hanoi, we flew to Da Nang where we got on a bus and drove the reverse of the previous trip, ending in Saigon.

In 2001 we made another flight to Hanoi, and working with a Vietnamese travel company made an excursion into the area where I believed I was shot down. It was definitely not the village where I was captured. Two years later we visited Vietnam again, this time with my Granddaughter. We made the trip up to Camp Dogpatch and did some touring in N. Vietnam, but didn't have any new leads on my shoot-down site.

Finally, in 2011, I invested the money and, working with a travel company in South Vietnam, hired a guide who was dependable and who had some good contacts in the Hanoi government. Once I paid the requisite bribes, everything fell into place. All the arrangements were made, and with my wife Barbie and daughter Ann, I traveled to Nhu Han Village. At the end of a rutted dirt road, it hadn't changed much in forty-five years. The inhabitants were still simple rice farmers, and they hadn't shown any anger or tried to mistreat us when we were first captured. They told me that we were the first Americans they had ever seen. Now they were curious why I would come there after all these years. I told them through the interpreter, 'I just want to thank you for not killing me.' They were appreciative. I had some gifts for them— school supplies for the school which I was held in after capture. It was a good experience. I was able to get closure on that chapter of my life."

Ken surrounded by students from Nhu Han school—45 years lat

Time to Celebrate!

Chapter 17

"Humble yourselves, therefore, under God's mighty hand, that he may lift you up in due time."
1 Peter: 5-6

What a world! Three months earlier, Major Cordier (having been promoted in prison) was still languishing in his Vietnamese prison cell. In Chapter 12 we saw him creatively making a small amount of alcohol using the raw materials at hand. Now, on May 24, 1973, here he was with his comrades-in-arms, sharing an elegant dinner and celebration with none other than President Richard Nixon!

Ken with wife Barbie, meeting with President Nixon during a POW reunion in Austin, TX in 1984.

As we've seen, President Nixon had escalated the war by bombing Hanoi and Haiphong for twelve consecutive nights, resulting in the Vietnamese returning to the Paris peace talks, the end of the war and the release of the POWs from their Asian hell-holes. Now here they were, celebrating with the likes of Bob Hope, John Wayne, Sammy Davis Jr., Ann Margaret and the President himself.

This was a party! It was a lavish affair with nearly 1,300 guests on the White House South Lawn; the largest dinner party ever held on the grounds of the White House before or since. A giant tent was erected to accommodate the crowd, with 126 round tables set up for the guests. The tent was longer and wider than the White House itself. The food was all-American, including sirloin steak, fingerling potatoes and strawberry mousse. There were 450 former POWs and their guests present. President Nixon called them "the most distinguished group I have ever addressed".

Louise Hutchinson of the *Chicago Tribune* was one of the guests. "It was an evening of prayer, of thanksgiving and now and then, of tears."[1] Irving Berlin performed his song 'God Bless America,' which warmed the hearts of all present, especially those who were eternally grateful to be home again with their families. When "the military honor guard brought in a tiny American flag and hung it on stage in a place of honor, the applause was deafening... it had been made in secret in a Vietnamese prison."[2]

Though the event came as Nixon was embroiled in the Watergate scandal, the just-freed POWs praised the President for his efforts to secure their freedom. "He was a hero to us," said former POW, Marine Capt. Orson Swindle. "He will always be revered by us as a group because he got us home when we didn't know how or if we were going to get home."

Retired U.S. Navy Captain Mike McGrath, 27 years old when his plane was shot down, remembers the glamour of the White House celebration and the President's gracious hospitality. "They gave the POWs the run of the White House, including their family quarters. The President and Mrs. Nixon said goodnight at midnight, but he invited us to stay and dance as long as we wished. What an evening, to dance until the band quits and have free run of the White House!"

The POW choir, made up of more than 30 former POWs, including Maj. Cordier, sang a 'hymn' written by one of Ken's fellow prisoners at the Zoo, Col. Quincy Collins. Here are the lyrics:

The POW Hymn

Oh God to Thee we raise a prayer and sing.
From within these foreign prison walls.
We're men who wear the gold and silver wings.
And proud, we heed our nation's call.
Give us strength to withstand,
All the harm at the hands of our enemy.
We pledge unswerving faith and loyalty,
To our cause, America, and to Thee. Amen.

What a difference to sing it here and now, instead of ever so carefully and quietly in their cells at the 'Hanoi Hilton'!

God was never forgotten during this magnificent celebration. Navy Capt. Charles G. Gillespie, the POW chaplain in N. Vietnam, gave a prayer with lots of thanks and praise to God who had brought them through it all, and eventually home. He ended with this: *"Oh Lord, as Thou has been with us during the time of our adversity, I pray that Thou will continue to be with us during this time of our prosperity. Even as Thou has not forsaken us during the years of our imprisonment, I pray that we will not forsake thee, during these years of our freedom. Let us live our lives so that the words of our mouths and the meditations of our hearts be always acceptable in Thy sight, Oh Lord, our strength and our Redeemer. Amen."*

114

Back to Work

Chapter 18

*"Let us not become weary in doing good, for at the
proper time we will reap a harvest if we do not give up."*
Galatians 6: 9

Once home, Ken would get back on his feet and become better than ever. Like Job from the Bible, who had everything taken away from him—his health, family, possessions, freedom-God restored it all and then some. After his four months of convalescent leave, he returned to active duty as a student at the Armed Forces Staff College in Norfolk, VA. Following that, he moved his family to Randolph AFB, TX where he requalified to fly jet aircraft. From there, he was assigned to Holloman A.F.B., NM, where he again flew Phantoms, as a Flight Commander and then Operations Officer.

In 1976, Col. Cordier was assigned to Headquarters, U.S. Air Forces in Europe (USAFE) at Ramstein AB, Germany, where he was Chief of the War Plans Division. He was responsible for writing and updating all conventional and nuclear war plans for employment of U.S. Air Forces in the European theater. This included planning the $800Mil conventional munitions stockpile for both Europe-based and contingency forces. The actual positioning and storage of munitions presented a dynamic challenge to ensure that the correct munitions would be on hand to accomplish each unit's mission in the event of hostilities. Col. Cordier pioneered the use of threat-based computer modeling to determine the optimum mix of munitions required at each airbase to support wartime tasking. This saved millions of dollars in repositioning costs and rationalized theater requirements with the existing worldwide conventional munitions stockpile and planned acquisitions.[1]

He became Deputy Commander for Operations at Sembach AB, Germany in 1979. He had met his future wife Barbie at the Ramstein Officer's Club and they were married in a 14th Century German church in June 1980, complete with a reception held in the local Gasthaus.

In 1981 he became the Base Commander of Wiesbaden Air Base in charge of the Base reactivation. The next year he was selected to be Air Attaché to the United Kingdom. They took up their new residence in London, at 41 Brompton Square, Knightsbridge. An Air Attaché is the liaison between our U.S. Air Force and the host nation, reporting directly to the U.S. Ambassador. This would be a very interesting and important job. Both Ken and Barbie attended the Defense Attaché school in Washington, D.C, which taught them the ins and outs of embassy life and operations, and the concept of the country team.

Exactly what does the Air Attaché do? "You build relationships with the host nation, and with your service counterparts, in my case, the Royal Air Force. You participate in ceremonial functions and military events. You host social gatherings for the host nation and foreign military personnel. You are expected to write status reports and of course it was made easier because of our close relationship with the United Kingdom. I didn't have to gather information surreptitiously."

Col. Cordier advised the US Ambassador on all issues relating to the U.S. Air Force presence in-country, and acted as liaison between the Embassy and Third Air Force Headquarters at RAF Mildenhall, traveling throughout the country to observe and report on military facilities and activities. The Cordiers lived in London nearly three years in this position.

Colonel Cordier also maintained close coordination with the State Department on political-military issues during the politically sensitive period of the first Cruise Missile deployment. Daily professional and social contact with top Ministry of Defense officials and Senior RAF staff officers resulted in close relationships that greatly facilitated agreement on cooperative defense issues.

How does one get such a job? "I got promoted to Colonel, so I was looking for a career enhancing assignment. Several of the other POWs had become Attachés. That sounded appealing. It turned out that the Brits in the RAF wanted somebody with a fighter background, someone that they could work with. The officer I replaced was an academic, having taught at the Air Force Academy. He was a nice guy; however he had spent his whole career in academics. The RAF is primarily a fighter force so it was easier for them to work with someone with an operational background. Because I flew the F-4 and they had F-4's in their inventory, it was a really good fit."

It was a good fit for Barbie as well. Her exceptional people skills made her a natural for hosting frequent activities with dignitaries, diplomats, American senior military personnel and congressional visitors. They were also privileged to meet most of the British Royal family. Col. Cordier's outstanding performance as Air Attaché in London was recognized by the award of the Defense Superior Service Medal.

In 1985, he retired from the Air Force with a retirement ceremony at the famed Guildhall in London. The Cordiers then moved to Washington D.C., where Ken took a position with British Aerospace as their Marketing Director for military aircraft in North America. They lived on Capitol Hill for eight years, six blocks from the Capitol, on Maryland Avenue, NE.

In 1993 they moved to Dallas, where he has served in leadership positons in several national veterans' organizations. Now public speaking has become part of his priorities, and there is an increasing interest in his talks. Many vets deal with their feelings by trying to avoid the subject, and simply move on with their lives. Ken has found the opposite approach more helpful. As he says, "My way of dealing with it is talking about it, and sharing my story with various groups."

"For he acknowledges my name..."

Chapter 19

" 'Because he loves me,' says the LORD, 'I will rescue him; I will protect him, For he acknowledges my name. He will call on me, and I will answer him; I will be with him in trouble, I will deliver him and honor him. With long life I will satisfy him and show him my salvation.' " Psalm 91:14-16

"I was raised in a Protestant fundamentalist denomination as a child, and never questioned it. I was baptized at the age of thirteen when I accepted Christ as my personal Lord and Savior. While I never had a born again experience, I just kind of grew in the faith.

"I had a firm belief in God, without the necessity of describing Him in detail: an omnipotent, all-powerful God who is the Creator. God has no beginning and no end, so it's hard for us, with our four-pound brains, to get our mind around such a concept. I don't feel a need to describe in detail a lot of these things; I just step out on faith.

"Here's something to think about, regarding our need to describe God and Heaven. One day in Dallas, I was out on my morning walk. It was as clear as a bell, and I saw a jet fly over. He must have been at 40,000 feet. He was so high I could barely make out the outline of the airplane. It was pulling a vapor trail for several miles behind it, just straight as an arrow. There wasn't any wind up there, because it didn't disperse or blow this way and that. I thought, how would people in ancient times have described that, and what would they have thought it was, had they seen such a thing? So, that's how I feel about describing Heaven. It's another dimension that is not visible to us in this lifetime. Just believe in it, that's enough for me. There are many references to Heaven in the Bible and Randy Alcorn's book <u>Heaven</u> does a good job of trying it all together." [1]

Ken's story is replete with Biblical analogies and metaphors. We'll take a look at one last one here: Psalm 91.

"He who dwells in the shelter of the Most High
will abide in the shadow of the Almighty.
I will say to the LORD, "My refuge and my fortress,
my God, in whom I trust."
Psalm 91:1-2

The opening verses of this Psalm set the stage, and gave us the bottom line: trust in God, and He will be our strength and salvation. Good advice for trying times, such as the ones Ken found himself in. Thoughts about family and country may be comforting, but in the final analysis, the only thing that endures is God.

"For he will deliver you from the snare of the fowler
and from the deadly pestilence.
He will cover you with his pinions,
and under his wings you will find refuge;
his faithfulness is a shield and buckler."
Psalm 91:3-4

These two verses seem especially apropos to Ken's case. The snare of the fowler refers to the 'bird catcher's trap', and indeed Ken's wings were clipped when his F-4C Phantom was plucked out of the air and he was thrown into a cage.

It is significant that during his 75 month stay in Vietnam prisons, Ken never contracted any form of a 'deadly pestilence'. Not all of the POWs were so blessed. A few died of tropical disease such as yellow fever. The living conditions which the POWs endured made them especially vulnerable to disease.

First of all, Vietnam exists in a tropical climate, typically a breeding pot for such pestilences. The real culprits there are tropical diseases carried by mosquitoes, such as malaria, dengue

119

fever, encephalitis and yellow fever. Even with a mosquito net to sleep under at night, the local mosquitoes feasted on the POWs constantly during the day. To top it off, they all suffered from a significantly depressed immune system due to severe malnutrition, increasing weakness and unhygienic living conditions, leaving them all the more susceptible to contracting one of these life-threatening diseases. Ken noticed he was rapidly losing weight during the first six months, going from 160 pounds to an estimated 120 pounds, judging by his protruding shoulder bones, ribs and hips. They also were literally sharing their living space with the local rats, spiders and other poisonous critters that surrounded them 24/7.

Nonetheless, Ken has often said that he *never* doubted that he would eventually be saved from this hell-hole and return safely home. In the meantime, the only way they could be sheltered, would be under God's protective wings; as the eagle mightily protects her young.

One more health note here. When Ken was shot down, he broke his back. Once captured, he was forced to sleep on the floor of his cell. During his initial physical exam, he complained about this to the docs, but they shrugged and said it was probably the best 'treatment' for it, under the circumstances. X-rays showed that he has a 50% compression of his T-12 vertebrae.

"You will not fear the terror of the night,
nor the arrow that flies by day,
nor the pestilence that stalks in darkness,
nor the destruction that wastes at noonday.
A thousand may fall at your side,
ten thousand at your right hand,
but it will not come near you."
Psalm 91: 5-7

God puts a shield of protection around His beloved. And when pestilence and troubles assault us and assail us, we can count on

His covering and His protection. You might say, "Well, I know people who died in combat, accidents and disease. Where was their protection?"

Jesus said, "In this world you will have tribulation but be of good cheer, for I have overcome the world." Jesus also said, "Do not let your hearts be troubled. Trust in God; trust also in me. In my Father's house are many rooms; if it were not so, I would have told you. I am going there to prepare a place for you. And if I go and prepare a place for you, I will come back and take you to be with me that you also may be where I am." John 14:1-3

Whether in life or in death we are promised His protection. We are immortal in the will of God. "The world and its desires pass away, but whoever does the will of God lives forever." 1 John 2:17

Although we will not see the ultimate fulfillment of all of God's promises while here on earth, these last verses seem to be custom-designed for Ken while still here:

"Because he loves me," says the LORD, "I will rescue him;
I will protect him, for he acknowledges my name.
He will call on me, and I will answer him;
I will be with him in trouble,
I will deliver him and honor him."
Psalm 91:14-15

Ken has always acknowledged His name. And the Lord has always been with him. He called on God often to deliver him, and in His own time, He did so. Not that everything would be sunshine and roses once home. But He *would* honor him.

His combat decorations are many, including: the Silver Star with oak leaf cluster; the Legion of Merit; Distinguished Flying Cross; Bronze Star with combat "V" for Valor; Air Medal with 6 oak leaf clusters; the Prisoner of War Medal and the Purple Heart.

121

He also holds the Defense Superior Service Medal and 12 other U.S. and foreign awards and decorations.

America's fighter pilots are truly our guardian eagles, and have demonstrated exceptional service and bravery in all of America's wars where fighter aircraft were used. Their bravery has frequently been acknowledged with medals. Several medals can be earned, but the Silver Star is particularly designed "for conspicuous gallantry in action against an enemy of the United States". It is the third-highest military decoration for valor awarded to members of the United States Armed Forces.

An appropriate example is Captain Cordier's Nov. 11, 1966 mission where he earned his first Silver Star. Here's the official account of that day:

"The President of the United States of America, authorized by Act of Congress, July 8, 1918 (amended by act of July 25, 1963), takes pleasure in presenting the Silver Star to Captain Kenneth William Cordier (AFSN: 71351), United States Air Force, for gallantry in connection with military operations against an opposing armed force as an F-4C Pilot of the 559th Tactical Fighter Squadron, Cam Ranh Bay Air Base, Vietnam, PACIFIC Air Forces, in action in Southeast Asia, on 11 November 1966. On that date, Captain Cordier was the Mission Commander leading a flight against a target in North Vietnam. His first pass in the target area drew heavy hostile reaction and his wingmen were downed on their initial passes. Completely disregarding his own personal safety, Captain Cordier immediately initiated rescue procedures and delivered his remaining ordnance on the nearby target. Captain Cordier then remained in the area to provide assistance to inbound rescue aircraft until his low fuel state dictated his departure from the area. By his gallantry and devotion to duty, Captain Cordier has reflected great credit upon himself and the United States Air Force."

In addition to military honors, he has been awarded other high honors, including the prestigious National Society Daughters of the American Revolution Medal of Honor in 1998. This is the highest award presented by the DAR, and it was bestowed on Col. Cordier based upon his "demonstrated leadership, trustworthiness, patriotism and service to the local community and nation".

He was also presented the *Freedoms Foundation at Valley Forge* honor award in 1973. In 1985 he was selected by the American Fighter Aces Association as an honorary member. He was awarded the Sam Houston Medal presented by the Texas Grand Masonic Lodge. In 2003, he was inducted into the Combat Aviation Hall of Fame.

Today, he is a frequent speaker on his war time experiences. He is active in a number of Veteran's organizations, including being past President of the NAM POW National organization, past President of the Red River Valley Fighter Pilots association, twice Chairman of the Dallas Military Ball and Chairman of the Dallas Veterans Day Parade. Several other honors, too many to list here, have also been bestowed on him.

"With long life I will satisfy him
and show him my salvation."
Psalm 91:16

Having passed the 80 year milestone, Ken has often commented on what a blessed life he has lived. "Looking back on it, I look at that (POW) experience as a speed bump in life that I had to get over -- to enjoy the blessed life I've had ever since. And I've had a wonderful life." Amen!

THE END

Ken and Barbie Cordier at home in Dallas, Texas.

*"And after you have suffered a little while, the God of all grace,
who has called you to his eternal glory in Christ,
will himself restore, confirm, strengthen, and establish you."*
1 Peter 5:10

Footnotes

Preface

1. Mattel has sold over a billion Barbie dolls, making it the company's largest and most profitable line. Barbie was launched in March, 1959. Ken is a Mattel toy doll introduced in 1961 as the fictional boyfriend of toy doll Barbie. Over the years they took up many different roles and identities. Here's 'Air Force Ken and Barbie':

Prologue

1. From President John F. Kennedy's letter to Charles Callison of the National Audubon Society, July 18, 1961

2. For example: Ezekiel 17: 3, 2 Samuel 1:23, Exodus 19:4, Job 39:27, Daniel 7:4, Psalm 103:5, Revelation 8:13.

3. For example, He 'shadows us' (Psalm 36:7, 63:7, 91:1-4, 1st King 8:7), 'covers us' (Psalm 91:1-4), 'hides us' (Psalm 17:8) and is even 'under us' (Psalm 36). In Jewish thought, the eagle is the symbol of mercy (rachamim).

4. Mark Batterson, an American pastor and author, made an interesting remark on this subject, *"We live in a culture that overvalues 15 minutes of fame, and undervalues lifelong faithfulness."*

5. Here are some Biblical examples:
a) "Know therefore that the LORD your God is God; he is the faithful God, keeping his covenant of love to a thousand generations of those who love him and keep his commandments." Deut. 7:9

b) "For the word of the LORD is right and true; he is faithful in all he does." Psalm 33:4

c) "If we are faithless, he remains faithful, for he cannot disown himself." 2 Tim. 2:13

Mother Teresa said, *"God does not require that we be successful, only that we be faithful."*

Chapter 1 – "For Such a Time as This"

1. A boil is a skin abscess, i.e. a collection of pus that forms in the skin. It is often very painful. The skin around the boil becomes infected, turns red, painful, warm, and swollen. More boils may appear around the original one. A fever may develop and lymph nodes may become swollen. If you are in poor health, you may develop high fever and chills along with the infection, requiring quick medical attention. http://patient.info/health/abscess-leaflet

2. According to the CIA's 1963 KUBARK interrogation manual (KUBARK was a U.S. Central Intelligence Agency cryptonym for the CIA itself), obtained in 1997 by the *Baltimore Sun*, sensory deprivation was a measure long favored by the CIA, and considered effective for most of the life of the agency. http://www.salon.com/2007/06/07/sensory_deprivation. Research shows that Vitamin D deficiencies in men caused by insufficient sunlight make them *twice* as likely to develop heart disease. It can also lead to the development of prostate and breast cancer, memory loss, damage to the immune system, and an increased risk for developing dementia, schizophrenia and a form of clinical depression, Seasonal Affective Disorder (SAD). Symptoms can be extreme: mood swings, anxiety, sleep problems, or even suicidal thoughts.

3. Ibid. For particularly rapid results during interrogation, the KUBARK manual endorses the use of a "cell which has no light (or weak artificial light which never varies)." Those who spend an extended time at night

exposed to artificial lights have shown an inclination to the development of cancers, diabetes, heart disease, and obesity.

4. Trịnh Thị Ngọ (1931- 2016), a.k.a. "Hanoi Hannah ", became famous among US soldiers for these broadcasts on Radio Hanoi. There were actually several "Hanoi Hannahs", but she was the senior and most frequently heard one. She made three broadcasts a day, reading a list of the newly killed or imprisoned Americans, attempting to persuade US GIs that the US involvement in the Vietnam War was unjust and immoral, and playing popular US songs in an attempt to incite feelings of nostalgia and homesickness.

Here is an excerpt from one of her June 16, 1967 broadcasts: *"How are you, GI Joe? It seems to me that most of you are poorly informed about the going of the war, to say nothing about a correct explanation of your presence over here. Nothing is more confused than to be ordered into a war to die or to be maimed for life without the faintest idea of what's going on."*

5. Three examples:
a) *"For all have sinned and fall short of the glory of God, and all are justified freely by his grace through the redemption that came by Christ Jesus."* Romans 3:23-24

b) *"If we claim to be without sin, we deceive ourselves and the truth is not in us."* 1 John 1:8

c) *"For the wages of sin is death, but the gift of God is eternal life in Christ Jesus our Lord."* Romans 6:23

6. *"And I heard a loud voice from the throne saying, 'Behold, the dwelling place of God is with man. He will dwell with them, and they will be his people, and God himself will be with them as their God. He will wipe every tear from their eyes, and death shall be no more, neither shall there be no more, neither shall there be crying, nor pain anymore, for the former things have passed away."* Revelation 21: 1-4 (ESV)

7. Esther, an inconsequential Jewish orphan, who ended up Queen of the greatest pagan empire in the world (Persia, c. 450 B.C), saved her people from genocide, and so preserved the blood line of the coming Messiah, Jesus. From Jewish orphan to Queen, to savior of her people, to the birth of Jesus: an amazing and unlikely chain of events.

8. Three relevant verses:

a) *"This light momentary affliction is preparing for us an eternal weight of glory beyond all comparison, as we look not to the things that are seen but to the things that are unseen. For the things that are seen are transient, but the things that are unseen are eternal."* 2 Corinthians 4: 17-18

b) *"...through many tribulations we must enter the kingdom of God."* Acts 14:22

c) God *"comforts us in all afflictions, so that we may be able to comfort those who are in any affliction with the comfort which we ourselves are comforted by God."* 2 Corinthians 1:4

Chapter 2 - A Fun but Not So Easy Job

1. Brig. Gen. (Ret.) Gerald, E. McIlmoyle and Linda Rios Bromley, McDowell Publications, Utica, KY, 2008, p. 12

2. First published in the *South Carolina Aviation News*. http://www.globalaviator.co.za/Humour/aviationhumour.htm

3. Dialogue spoken from the opening sequence of each episode of *The Six Million Dollar Man* (ABC TV show, 1974 to 1978), starring Lee Majors.

4. As of June 30, 2013, there were 14,426 Air Force pilots of rank LtCol and lower. Those above this rank are overwhelmingly in non-flying leadership positions. (Tracy Bryan, *Quora*, https://www.quora.com/How-many-fighter-pilots-are-there-in-the-US). There are also fighter pilots present in the U.S. Navy and Army.

5. As of 2014, an increasing shortage of Air Force fighter pilots existed. http://www.airforcetimes.com/story/military/careers/air-force/2015/03/20/fighter-pilot-shortage-air-force/25033413/*Air Force Times*

6. Depicted in *Independence Day*, Harry Connick, Jr. plays Captain Jimmy Wilder who, while pushing his jet beyond his physical limits, passes out, and then is quickly destroyed by aliens.

7. FoxNewsPolitics, http://www.foxnews.com/politics/2013/07/26/air-force-facing-fighter-pilot-shortage-offers-retention-bonuses-up-to-225000.html, July 26, 2013

8. According to the Government Accountability Office pay chart in 2016.

9. Twain, Mark, *Roughing It*, Chapter XXII, 1886.

10. A Minuteman missile could stand ready for extended periods of time with little maintenance, and then launch on command. This potential for immediate launch gave the missile its name; like the Revolutionary War's Minutemen, the Minuteman was designed to be launched on a moment's notice. Minuteman entered service in 1962 as a weapon tasked primarily with the deterrence role. Peaking at 1,000 in the 1970s, the current U.S. force consists of 450 missiles. Wikipedia

11. The *Hanoi Hilton* (Hỏa Lò Prison) was a prison used in Vietnam for political prisoners, and later by North Vietnam for U.S. Prisoners of War during the Vietnam War. During this later period it was sarcastically known to American POWs as the Hanoi Hilton. It was one site used by the North Vietnamese Army to house, interrogate and torture captured Americans, mostly American pilots shot down during bombing raids.

12. The McDonnell Douglas F-4 Phantom II served as the principal air superiority fighter for both the Navy and Air Force during the Vietnam War. As a large fighter, it could carry more than 18,000 pounds of weapons, with a top speed of over Mach 2 (approximately 1,675 miles per hour). It set 15 world records for in-flight performance beginning in 1959, including absolute speed and altitude records.

Chapter 3 – "Eject!"

1. A 'back-seater' is a weapon systems operator ("WSO", pronounced "wizzo"). The WSO integrates with the pilot to collectively achieve and maintain crew efficiency, situational awareness and mission effectiveness. Wikipedia

Cut away view of the front and rear cock pits.
A mass of sophisticated panels, buttons, screens, levers and controls.

2. A surface-to-air missile (SAM) is a missile designed to be launched from the ground to destroy aircraft or other missiles. The Vietnam War was the first modern war in which guided antiaircraft missiles seriously challenged highly advanced supersonic jet aircraft. It would also be the first and only time that the latest and most modern air defense technologies of the Soviet Union and the most modern jet fighter planes and bombers of the United States confronted each other in combat. Nearly 17,000 Soviet missile technicians and operator/instructors deployed to North Vietnam in 1965 to help defend Hanoi against American bombers, while North Vietnamese missile men completed their six to nine months of SAM training in the Soviet Union.

From 1965 through 1966, nearly all of the 48 U.S. jet aircraft shot down by SAMs over North Vietnam were downed by Soviet missile men. Col. Cordier was probably one of these, as he was shot down on December 2, 1966.

The Soviet Union supplied 7,658 SAMs to North Vietnam, and their defense forces conducted about 5,800 launches, usually in multiples of three. By the early 1960s, the deployment of SAMs had rendered high-speed high-altitude flight in combat practically suicidal.

3. Joseph's amazing story is told in Genesis 37-50.

4. Joseph's "robe of many colors", was a special coat made just for him by his Father. To his brothers, it showed that *"their father loved him more than all his brothers"*...and so... *"they hated him and could not speak peacefully to him."* (Exodus 37: 3-4) Ken's special apparel was provided by the USAF. A flight suit is a full body garment. These suits are generally made to keep the wearer warm, as well as being practical (multiple pockets with closures of buttons, snaps, or zippers to prevent loss of articles during maneuvers) and durable (including being fire retardant). A military flight suit may also show rank insignia.

5. Forward Air Controllers (FACs) flew day and night in low slow aircraft performing aerial reconnaissance for both US and Allied Forces, directed air strikes in support of embattled ground units, interdicted enemy infiltration routes, and coordinated rescue operations.
http://www.fac-assoc.org.
http://www.vietnamwar50th.com/forward_air_controllers_association,

6. The Việt Cộng was the name given by Western sources to the NLF (National Liberation Front) during the Vietnam War (1955-1975). The NLF was a political organization in South Vietnam and Cambodia that had its own army: the PLAF (People's Liberation Armed Forces of South Vietnam) .

The People's Liberation Armed Forces of South Vietnam (PLAF)'s best-known action was the 1968 Tet Offensive, a massive assault on more than 100 South Vietnamese urban centers, including an attack on the U.S. embassy in Saigon. The offensive riveted the attention of the world's media for weeks, but also overextended the Việt Cộng. Later communist offensives were conducted predominantly by the North Vietnamese.

7. MiG aircraft are a staple of the Soviet and Russian air forces, and the Soviet Union sold many of these aircraft within its sphere of influence. They have been used by the militaries of China, North Korea, and North Vietnam in aerial confrontations with American and allied forces, and now form part of the air forces of many Arab nations. https://en.wikipedia.org/wiki/Mikoyan

8. An electronic counter measure (ECM) is an electronic device designed to deceive radar, sonar or other detection systems, like infrared (IR) or lasers. The system may make many separate targets appear to the enemy, or make the real target seem to disappear or move about randomly. It is used effectively to protect aircraft from guided missiles. Most air

forces use ECM to protect their aircraft from attack. https://en.wikipedia.org/wiki/Electronic_countermeasure

9. An inertial navigation system (INS) is a navigation aid that uses a computer, motion sensors (accelerometers) and rotation sensors (gyroscopes) to continuously calculate via dead reckoning the position, orientation, and velocity (direction and speed of movement) of a moving object without the need for external references. It is used on vehicles such as ships, aircraft, submarines, guided missiles, and spacecraft. https://en.wikipedia.org/wiki/Inertial_navigation_system

10. American military are known to have totaled 725 taken prisoner during the Vietnam War. Almost 500 of these were downed pilots or airmen. By the war's end, about 205 aircraft had been lost to North Vietnamese surface-to-air missiles. Not counting helicopter pilots and air crewmen, over 6,000 Fixed-wing/propeller/jet US pilots and air crewmen were killed or missing during the Vietnam War. Among fixed-wing aircraft, more F-4 Phantoms were lost than any other type in service with any nation.

11. Barbie Cordier, interview of April 4, 2016.

Chapter 4 - The Breaking Point

1. Col. Ken Cordier, *Never give up. Never give in.* YouTube video: https://www.youtube.com/watch:v=mIKsWOFgRzQVeteranTalesProject.com, November 2, 2013.

2. Mohandas Karamchand Gandhi (1869 – 1948) was the preeminent leader of the Indian independence movement in British-ruled India. Employing nonviolent civil disobedience, Gandhi led India to independence and inspired movements for civil rights and freedom across the world. He is unofficially called the Father of the Nation.

3. http://middleeast.about.com/od/iraq/ig/Abu-Ghraib-Torture-Photos/Inmates-and-underwear.htm.

4. http://www.merriam-webster.com/dictionary/torture

5. Farrell, John Aloysius'. *A Refining Experience, The Boston Globe*, January 1, 2000

6. Leon Panetta, the CIA director, has confirmed that controversial 'enhanced interrogation techniques' such as waterboarding yielded some of the intelligence information that ultimately led to Osama bin Laden."
http://www.telegraph.co.uk/news/worldnews/al-qaeda/8491509/Osama-bin-Laden-killed-CIA-admits-waterboarding-yielded-vital-information.html

7. Hubbell, John G. (1976). *P.O.W.: A Definitive History of the American Prisoner-Of-War Experience in Vietnam*, 1964–1973. New York: Reader's Digest Press, ISBN 0-88349-091-9, p. 548.

8. Lieut. Commander John S. McCain III, United States Navy (1973-05-14), *"How the POW's Fought Back"*, U.S. News & World Report. Reposted under title *"John McCain, Prisoner of War: A First-Person Account"*, January 28, 2008.

9. Mahler, Jonathan (December 25, 2005). *"The Prisoner"*. The New York Times Magazine.

10. Thorsness, Leo (June 7, 2009). *"Surviving Torture"*. The Philadelphia Inquirer. Archived from the original on June 30, 2009.

11. Farrell, John Aloysius'. *A Refining Experience,* The Boston Globe, January 1, 2000; also see https://en.wikipedia.org/wiki/U.S._Prisoners_of_War_during_the_Vietnam_War.

12. Jeremiah Andrew Denton, Jr. (1924-2014) was a Rear Admiral and Naval Aviator in the United States Navy and later an U.S. Senator representing Alabama. As a Naval pilot during the Vietnam War, Denton is widely known for having been shot down over enemy territory — and for enduring almost eight years under grueling conditions as a prisoner of war in North Vietnam. https://en.wikipedia.org/wiki/Jeremiah_Denton.

Chapter 5 – Solitary Man

1. Neil Diamond's hit song "Solitary Man" was released in April, 1966. Ironically, Captain Cordier did his month of solitary just a few

months after its release. It is possible that Hanoi Hannah was playing this song on her radio show while Captain Cordier was playing a real solitary man.

2. The POWs gave him the nickname 'The Rabbit' because of his ears. Before Ken had heard this moniker, he'd given him one of his own: Alfred E. Newman. See any resemblance?

The Rabbit

Alfred E. Newman (What? Me Worry?)

3. "Extended periods of solitary confinement were a unique aspect of the Vietnam POW experience. Social isolation has been rated by the POWs themselves (Ray Vohden, 1974) as one of the three most important sources of stress in captivity. The stress engendered by solitary confinement was exceeded only by the amount of stress produced by the event of capture itself and the stress which resulted from physical torture during captivity. (Hunter, 1976)." *Stress Disorders Among Vietnam Veterans: Theory, Research, and Treatment*, Edited by Rigley Ph.D., Routledge Taylor & Francis Group, New York, 1978, p. 194.

4. In 1842 Charles Dickens made a visit to Eastern Penitentiary in Philadelphia, known popularly as "Cherry Hill". After seeing some of the consequences, he made an interesting comment regarding solitary confinement: *"I believe that very few men are capable of estimating the immense amount of torture and agony which this dreadful punishment ... inflicts upon the sufferers; and in guessing at it myself, and in reasoning from what I have seen written upon their faces, and what to my certain knowledge they feel within, I am only the more convinced that there is a depth of terrible endurance in it which none but the sufferers themselves can fathom, and which no man has a right to inflict upon his fellow-creature. I hold this slow and daily tampering with the mysteries of the brain, to be immeasurably worse than any torture of the body."* Charles Dickens, from his travelogue, *"American Notes for General Circulation"*, 1842.

Chapter 6 - Interrogators, Tormentors, and other Prison Staff

1. Lauri Halse Anderson, *The Impossible Knife of Memory* Reprint edition (June 2, 2015), Speak Publishers, 2014.

Chapter 7 – Prison Daze

1. Kallestad, Walt, *Christian Faith: The Basics*, Augsburg Press, Minneapolis, MN, p. 53

2. Ms. Bronte was an English novelist and poet, whose novels have become classics of English literature.

3. This song, written by Barry Mann & Cynthia Weil, first began being heard in Vietnam in the summer of 1966. By the next year it was the most requested song from military personnel, and was frequently requested and played by the American Forces Vietnam Network disc jockeys. Hanoi Hannah also played it often during her propaganda show.

4. Aeschylus (525 BC – 456 BC) was the earliest of the three greatest Greek tragedians, the others being Sophocles and Euripides.

5. Adolf Hitler, *Mein Kampf*, vol. I, ch. X.

Chapter 8 - The Cost of Freedom

1. James Bond Stockdale (1923 – 2005) was a United States Navy vice admiral, and a Medal of Honor recipient. He was a Vietnamese prisoner of war for over seven years.
2. *Newsweek*, February 26, 1973.

Chapter 11 – Son Tay Raid

1. John Gargus participated in the planning phase of the Son Tay rescue, and also flew as a lead navigator for the strike force. John Gargus, *The Son Tay Raid: American POWs in Vietnam Were Not Forgotten*, Williams-Ford Texas A&M University Military History Series, 2007.
2. In this painting, a USAF/Sikorsky HH-3E Jolly Green Giant helicopter from 37th Aerospace Rescue and Recovery Squadron has intentionally crash-landed inside the prison compound at 0219 to insert the BLUE BOY element of Green Berets. (Sơn Tây Raiders Association)
3. Murphy's Law states: "Anything that can go wrong, will go wrong."
4. John Gargus, *The Son Tay Raid: American POWs in Vietnam Were Not Forgotten*, Williams-Ford Texas A&M University Military History Series, 2007.

Chapter 13 - Beginning of the End

1. Air Force and Navy commanders and pilots were relieved that Nixon (unlike LBJ) left the operational planning to local commanders and loosened the targeting restrictions that had hampered Operation Rolling Thunder. By April 12, President Nixon informed Henry Kissinger that he had decided on a more comprehensive bombing campaign.

Chapter 14 – 'Operation Homecoming'

1. Historian Andrew H. Lipps captured the magnitude of such a moment in his account: *Operation Homecoming: The Return of American POWs from Vietnam*, http://archive.defense.gov/news/newsarticle.aspx?id=119272

Chapter 15 - *"Thank God Almighty. We're Free at Last!"*

1. Speech by Martin Luther King, Jr., during the march on Washington for Jobs and Freedom, August 28, 1963.

2. The song "Tie a Yellow Ribbon Round the Ole Oak Tree" is a song by Tony Orlando and Dawn, released in February, 1973. It reached number one in the US charts for four weeks in April, 1973.

3. Paul Fattig, *Coming Home, Medford Mail Tribune*, February. 13, 2013.

Chapter 16 - Homeward Bound

1. *"Stress Disorders Among Vietnam Veterans: Theory, Research and Treatment"* Charles R. Figley, Routledge, Taylor and Francis Group, London and New York, 1978, p. 194.

2. From a speech by Lt. Gen. Barry R. McCaffrey, (reproduced in the *Pentagram*, June 4, 1993) assistant to the Chairman of the Joint Chiefs of Staff, to Vietnam veterans and visitors gathered at "The Wall" Memorial.

3. Association for Psychological Science (APS), *The Graying of Trauma: Revisiting Vietnam's POWs*, http://www.psychologicalscience.org/index.php/news/were-only-human/the-graying-of-trauma-revisiting-vietnams-pows.html, accessed July 26, 2016.

4. Ibid.

5. TASK & PURPOSE, *The Shifting Public Perception of America's Veterans*, Jason Nulton, May 14, 2015.

6. This is a contested quote, with some sources calling it legitimate and accurate, and others denying it. See *The Wall Street Journal*, "How North Vietnam Won the War", 3 August 3, 1995, p. A8; and http://www.snopes.com/quotes/giap.asp;

7.Ibid.

8. Quote widely attributed to Nelson Mandela, however unable to identify exact source.

9. Ken Cordier, The East Texas War and Memory Project, Interviewer Nick Sprenger, February, 2014.

Chapter 17 - Time to Celebrate!

1. *The Chicago Tribune*, Louise Hutchinson, "Joy, Tears Mingle at POW Dinner", May 25, 1973.

2. Ibid.

Chapter 18 – Back to Work

1. https://en.wikipedia.org/wiki/Kenneth_Cordier, Wikipedia

Chapter 19 – "For He Acknowledges My Name"

1. The importance of belief runs all through Scripture. Here are three examples of its pre-eminence:

"For God so loved the world, that he gave his one and only son, that whoever believes in him shall not perish but have eternal life."
                                                              John 3:16
"Believe in the Lord Jesus, and you will be saved." Acts 16:31

"Jesus said to her, 'I am the resurrection and the life, he who believes in me will live, even though he dies. Do you believe this?'"
John 11:25-26

There are many others, e.g. Genesis 15: 6, Psalm 106: 12, Mark 5: 35-37, Mark 9: 23, Mark 16: 15-16, John 3: 18, John 5: 24, Romans 10: 8-9. When belief is spoken of in the Bible, it is talking about belief in the God of the Bible, and His only Son, Jesus. Not faith in yourself, another person, a cause, religion, nation, idea, force, another deity or anything else.

Acknowledgements

I am grateful to Chris Snidow for his tireless efforts to organize my scattered notes, speeches, and other inputs in a coherent manuscript. Chris has authored two books of his own and is a master of research and documentation. He has been an inspiration, keeping me focused and on track—no small thing. In fact, if it wasn't for Chris, this story may not have been written at all. His concept of my story in light of Biblical principles transformed it into my testimony rather than just another war story

To my loving wife Barbie goes my heartfelt thanks for her dedication and passion to see this project through to publication. She spent countless hours discussing content and pertinent parts of the story. My sister-in-law Nancy did a nice job of proofreading and editing through new eyes; thank you, Nance.

To the artist who presented me with her painting of an eagle in flight gear in front of an F-4C, Cher Jiang, my sincere thanks for providing the perfect cover depicting a Guardian Eagle.

My sincere thanks go to Col. Elmo 'Mo' Baker, USAF (Ret.) who generously gave of his time and advice on the mechanics of writing a book like this. Mo was a fellow POW who has written an excellent account of his experiences in prison, *Serve with Pride & Return with Honor.*

Finally, to my best friend in prison who I lived with through the bad times longer than any other POW, Capt. John M. "Mike McGrath, USN (Ret.). His personal pen and ink sketches from his book *Prisoner of War, Six Years in Hanoi*, published by the Naval Institute Press, illustrated some of the more graphic images from our POW experience. As NAM POW historian, Mike has kept the records on the POWs through his "Mac's Facts" and was eminently available when I had questions about times and places.